Mary Rogers Clendenin
Sept. 27-1934

WORKING WITH GOD

By
GARDNER HUNTING

UNITY SCHOOL OF CHRISTIANITY
KANSAS CITY, MO.
1934

WORKING WITH GOD
Is Dedicated

To those who never have tried it;

To those who think they have tried it, with poor results;

To those who think His promises are "too good to be true";

To those who perchance need only a challenge to put them to the test.

Nothing is too wonderful to be true.—FARADAY

Fear not, only believe.
It is your Father's good pleasure
to give you the kingdom.
                —JESUS

CONTENTS

Dedication	3
The Come-Back	7
Any Job You Want	23
Obedience to Law	29
Keeping the Whole Law	34
Learning to Love	45
Open Channel	51
Thinking about Thinking	60
Ideas in Trust	76
Self-Expression	83
Waiting	93
Holy or Human?	99
Shall We Be Different?	103
Real or Counterfeit	108
Maps and Instructions	114
Successful Trusting	120
Good "Bad" News	126
Harvest	132
My Own Will Come to Me	138
When I Am Unaware——	143
You Can't Beat Spiritual Law	149
"Now Is the Accepted Time"	154

The Come-Back

WHY NOT HAVE what you want? Have you settled down with a notion that you can't get it?

Are you accepting a disappointment as something you *must* suffer?

Do you look at the thing that you really desire as being far beyond your reach?

Do you carry around with you a heartache because you think your heart's desire is finally and forever denied you?

Do you look on yourself as being down and out, with no chance to get back?

Do you think you are too poor to buy the things you like or even the things you need?

Have you done something that you think has brought a penalty on you—sickness, poverty, loss of freedom, grief?

Well, before you give it all up as hopeless won't you just read along a little way in this discussion to see if your case is as bad as you think it is? I am not writing to sell you anything or to teach you anything or to persuade you of anything, but just to share with you the ideas that changed the life of a man who used to think as you do and who thought he had good reason to think so, but who has found out that he was mistaken and that life is not hopeless at all; and who believes that what helped him may help somebody else who is under a cloud similar to the one that he once lived under. Many things you want most are now within your reach.

It has been said that if a man were to offer twenty-dollar gold pieces for sale on the street at fifty cents each, there would be few buyers, because nearly everybody would leap to the conclusion that he was a fraud. If you will study the real reason why people instinctively feel that way, you will find in it the very secret of success in getting what *you* want.

You have heard it said a thousand times that "you can't get something for nothing." You may or may not think that you believe this to be true, but it is true, whether you believe it or not; and everybody deep down in his inner nature knows it is true. That's why he is shy of any promise that promises too much. That's why you are probably skeptical about the promise of this little piece of print. But just let this idea get a foothold in your mind: If it is a law that I cannot get something for nothing, then it must be true of this law, as it is of all genuine laws, that it works both ways; it must be true that *I cannot give anything without getting something for it.* Ever think of that?

Have you ever been surprised to find that when you liked or disliked a man or a woman, that person was sure to return the feeling you had for or "gave" to him? Have you ever noticed what a railroad company does that enables it to take in money? It gives transportation that is needed by people. Have you ever wondered why Henry Ford and John D. Rockefeller are so rich? Whatever else you may think of them, you must see that the world gives them money because they give something to the world—the one, a good low-priced car; the other, good oil at a reasonable price. What does a department store do before it gets regular customers? It gives service, courtesy, good will, a square deal, accommodation, and so forth, to a community, which brings in the trade as the direct and inevitable result. What does an employee do before he gets wages or a salary? He gives a day's work or a week's or a month's. What gets him a raise? Giving a little more than he is paid for, nothing else. What does a farmer do before he gets a crop? He gives the seed to the ground and gives it water and care. How does an artist or a writer win fame? By giving the world a work of art or some great literature. How do I win a friend? By giving him friendship, and in no other way.

Sometimes people say—and maybe you are one of them just now—that there are people who get something for nothing; who give nothing for what they receive. Did you ever study such cases or do you take somebody else's word for it, as most of us do in such matters? Well, are you from Missouri? If you honestly want to be shown, you are on the only sound ground that there is.

Now, who gets something for nothing? The man who finds an oil well in his back yard? The woman who marries a rich man? The miner who stumbles upon gold? The fellow who wins in the lottery? The thief who takes a purse or the contents of a bank vault? The swindler who cheats the unwary out of his property? The real estate shark who sells worthless lots for big prices? The bootlegger who makes his own liquor with wood alcohol, puts bogus labels on it, and sells it as "just off the ship"? The heirs who destroy the old will or forge a new one so that all the property comes to them? The counterfeiter who makes hundred-dollar bills out of mere paper and ink? The chap who raises a thousand-dollar check to $10,000? Do all—or any—of these get something for nothing? I used to think they did. Often it looks so.

But the more you watch the individuals who do these things, the more you'll see that the law works with them just as it works with you and me. It's law—just as truly as the law of gravitation is law—and I can't break it. Neither can you. Neither can anybody else. Did you ever know a gambler who got rich? Did you ever know a burglar who had anything left after his pals, his fence, and his lawyers got through with him? Did you ever know a counterfeiter who had cars and a country home and a yacht? Did you ever know a woman who married for money and was happy?

"Maybe not," you say, "but they got away with the profits of the crooked deal!" Did they? How long did the profits last? Do you *know?*

Did you ever know anybody to keep the money he won in a lottery? Did you ever know the "lucky" finder of oil or gold, who hadn't given something for it, to profit by it?

If you will let go of the rumors and fabulous stories about riches' coming to people for nothing, and get right down and investigate, you'll be surprised. Study the history of "depressions."

What is success in business made of? I mean any success in any business. Some persons will say, "Hard work." But that is not always true. Hard work alone will not insure success. You know plenty of persons who have worked hard but have gotten almost nothing for it. Does honesty make success? Not necessarily. Does dishonesty pay? No! Terribly upsetting, isn't it, to be told that neither crookedness nor honesty succeeds? Well, that's where you and I have been making a mistake. We have swung like pendulums from one extreme to the other. First we've tried to succeed by one method, then by the other. When crookedness fails, men preach honesty; when honesty fails, the preachers are dumbfounded and other men turn bitterly back to crookedness. What is the reason? Simply that neither mere dishonesty nor mere honesty pays; nor mere laziness, nor mere hard work. Nothing really pays but obedience to law—not man's law but God's law.

Gravitation is one of God's laws, isn't it? Who uses the law of gravitation? Anybody? Does it make any difference whether he is good or bad, honest or dishonest, crooked or straight, saint or sinner, rich or poor, fat or lean, white or black? It does not; the law of gravitation works for him infallibly, invariably, inflexibly, eternally, regardless of who or what he is. Who uses the laws governing the burning of gasoline to drive a car? Who uses the laws of friction to stop a car? Who uses the laws of electricity? the laws of light? Does it make any difference whether one is handsome or homely, whether he is freckled or pallid, whether he smokes or drinks or swears or goes to church or fights or steals or kills or loves? It does not. A murderer can drive a car or stop it. A clown can ride in an airplane. A fool can start or stop a dynamo. An idiot can set a fire. A preacher or a moron can explode dynamite. A sister of charity or a woman of the street will burn a hand on a hot stove. Good or bad, saintly or vicious—law works alike for all, and everything works under law.

But some laws seem to be greater than others, to include others, to transcend others. For instance, the laws controlling the airplane seem to enable us to break the law of gravitation. Of course, they don't; they simply enable us to counteract the force of gravitation. The laws of the radio release us from conditions to which we have thought ourselves limited by other governing laws —laws of sound transmission. By studying these things I see that so soon as I begin working by *any* law I begin to benefit by it, and no other law can stop me; because all the laws of nature fit together, work together, help one another—they never work against one another. The law of gravitation helps me to use the airplane, it holds me down against the air. If it did not, I'd be flung off the world into space, airplane and all—not to mention other things that would happen. When I start my car, the laws governing the action of the engine seem to overcome the laws of inertia and friction—but no law is broken. If it weren't for inertia there would be no momentum; if it weren't for friction my clutch would not grip and my tires would not take hold of the road. I do not break laws; I use them.

Now, a law that works at all always works. You say conditions affect laws? No; fog, for instance, only obscures the light of the stars to my eyes—the stars still shine. Static interferes with the radio only as it obscures the broadcasting for me; the broadcasting is there just the same. Law *always* works—anywhere—everywhere—now and forever. Two and two make four, by mathematical law, in New York or Kansas City, in Paris or Tokio, in the cathedral or the prison, in the home or the dive, on earth or Mars, today or in Cæsar's time, now or in eternity.

If this law that I cannot get something for nothing, and that therefore I cannot give without receiving, is law, then it works with the same infallibility and continuity as all other laws. It makes no difference who I am, where I am, how much I weigh, what color my hair is, or what my character is, this law works for me just the same.

It is commonly called the law of giving and receiving, and it can be stated this way: What I give out comes back to me—multiplied—always. The "come-back" is like the yield from seed.

Now, if you agree so far, don't you see where this has led you? It has led you to recognize that you are where you are today because of what you have given out. You are getting it back multiplied, just as I'm getting mine. But what else does it mean? It also means that what you start giving out now is also going to start coming back to you—multiplied. You can change the crop you are reaping, but there's just one way to do it: you can change the seed you are planting—change the sort of thing you are giving out. I did. It works, and nobody can stop it; nothing can stop it, no circumstance, no apparent handicap, no apparent misfortune, no "bad luck," no enemy, nobody who "has it in for you." What you give out comes back to you—what you begin giving out begins coming back to you. Any man, woman, or child can transform his life by transforming the thing he gives out.

Of course the first question that comes up in your mind (it was the first in my mind) is "How long must I suffer for what I've already done?" That's an interesting point. Suppose we think a minute about law: If I am working a problem in arithmetic, and I have been getting the wrong answer over and over and over again; and if I suddenly find that I've been trying to work the problem by the wrong method—contrary to

The Come-Back

principle—in opposition to law; and if I stop going contrary to law and work with law, how long does it take me to get the right answer? Suppose that I am learning to drive a car, and I try to start it by stepping on the gas without shifting into gear; the car does not start. But when I shift into gear—in other words obey the law governing the case—and then "step on the gas," how long does it take the car to start? Suppose I have a boat with a hole in it; I find that when I put it into the water, it fills and sinks. Suppose that I obey the law governing boats, and stop the leak; how long does it take the boat to float? If I am locked in a room and don't know how to unlock the door, I stay there till I learn how, do I not? But when I learn how to turn the key in that lock, how soon do I get out?

You may think out as many other examples as you like of how law works for you the moment you begin to obey it, of how obedience *now* cancels the mistakes of yesterday, or of last year. Then come back to our argument and think this one over: So true and far-reaching and fundamental is this law of giving and receiving that it extends into our thoughts. There's a lot of talk these days about the power of thought, and some persons are disposed to sneer at it. But there's more in it than these persons suppose, and they suffer because they don't realize the power of thought. It is true, too, that what you think comes back to you, multiplied. Is there a laugh in that for you? Well, can you do anything without first thinking about it? Is any discovery or invention, any work of art or book, any newspaper or tool, any manufacturing or any crime, any deed good or bad ever performed without some one's first thinking about it? In other words, everything that you do is first an idea in your mind. That is where it is first "created." If you make a chair, or a plan, or a steamship, or a printing press, or a bomb, or a broom, it must first take shape in your mind, as an idea. As a matter of fact, the idea of a thing is the real creation of it; the physical putting it together afterward is a mere copy of the idea in your mind.

We are accustomed to think that a certain amount of time and energy is required to make the visible copy of the idea—the visible chair, or plow, or broom. But the more perfectly we think it out—that is, create it as a complete idea in mind—the more quickly and perfectly we can create it in visible form; and as we think it out better and better, we find that we require less and less time to make the visible thing—and less and less energy. Newly invented machines, for instance, are usually crude, cumbersome, heavy, and require a lot of power to operate them. But as they are perfected—that is, as they are thought out—they become lighter, simpler, more efficient, are operated by less power, and do their work more quickly. In this process the time always comes when the thing that once took a long period and much labor to make is made at a speed so high that the production is in some cases almost instantaneous. If, when we began making this thing we had understood all the laws of its making, we could have made it instantaneously without going through the process of learning how.

But that would have been a miracle! Exactly! The difference between what we call a natural process and what we call a miracle is largely a matter of the time required to reach the desired end. But doing a "miracle" is merely a matter of understanding the laws by which it is done. The first Ford car required months of grueling labor to build; today the Ford plants can make about five and one half cars a minute—or one about every ten seconds. Is that a miracle? Wouldn't it have been a miracle to produce a Ford every ten seconds, say thirty years ago? What makes it possible today? Knowledge of the laws.

Knowledge of the laws involved in anything is not only the most valuable knowledge that we can have but it is absolutely essential. Mr. Ford never would have made a car if he had started with no knowledge of the law. But he began by using what he had—probably by using something that he had been told, or had read, about the laws of mechanics. As he used the knowledge that he had, his knowledge grew—just as your muscle grows as you use it—or as intelligence grows by use—or anything else. And wouldn't Henry Ford have been foolish not to try out his first bits of knowledge about law?

Think this over and you'll see that anything men ever achieve is accomplished by knowledge of the law. Health, wealth, happiness, success, prosperity, freedom! Anything you want literally will come to you if you will obey its laws just as literally as you obey the law of gravitation.

Now, of course you see the direction of this argument. A man's work or a woman's work is not primarily to do something hard that brings the sweat, breaks the nails, tires the muscles, and exhausts the wind—something that is drudgery. Not at all. The secret of getting what you want lies in obeying the law governing getting what you want.

What is that law? Why, it is just what we've been talking about—the law of giving and receiving.

Now, what is your first thought at this suggestion? You think, "What have I to give?" Perhaps you conclude that you have nothing. But Henry Ford had nothing—at the start—nothing but an idea. Heinz, the pickle man, of "fifty-seven varieties" fame, had nothing at the start—nothing but an idea. Woolworth, the five-and-ten-cent store man, had nothing at the start—nothing but an idea. Golden Rule Nash, the tailor, who built a business up from nothing to $12,000,000 in six years, had nothing at the start—nothing but an idea. But the curious thing about it is that these men all had the same idea. What was it? It was the idea of giving the world something that it needed—something of value. When they began acting on the idea by giving what they had to begin with, they learned how to give more, and so received more; and when they gave that, more came—until every one of them reached the point where he was successful and famous, and money rolled in upon him faster than he could use it.

It will work for you—this law. It has worked for me. It is working for you and for me whether we know it or not—whether we believe it or not. What you give out comes back to you—multiplied. If you don't get what you want, it's nobody's fault but your own. If I don't get what I want, it's nobody's fault but mine. The law works. If it works for me slowly at first, that is because I must learn by giving what I have, before I can get more knowledge of the law and thus have more to give. But if I will give what I have, where I am, to some one who needs it, I'll gain the knowledge and the things that I need. As I go on giving, I rapidly rise toward the point where I shall do easily and instantaneously the thing that now takes me a long time to do—just as my hand gains skill and speed and ease with a hammer, or a drill, or a needle, or a baseball, or a boxing glove, or a hoe, or a tennis racket, or a camera, or a motor car, or a dynamo. Eventually, by using all the knowledge I have of law, in giving service to the world, I shall gain the ability to do seeming miracles—as Henry Ford, Ty Cobb, Wm. Tilden, Barney Oldfield, Mary Pickford, Thomas Edison, and Luther Burbank have done.

If you believe that the foregoing argument is sound, has it occurred to you that the conclusion is not new? It's at least as old as the year 33

A. D. In other words, it has been taught to the world more or less ever since the time of Jesus Christ. In fact it was and is His teaching. Many people overlook the real teaching of Jesus of Nazareth. But listen: Didn't He say, "Give and it shall be given unto you, good measure, pressed down, shaken together and running over"? Whatever you think about Him religiously, did He know what He was talking about? Did He state a law?

We believe that Jesus of Nazareth did not merely found a religion, but that He taught a way to live—to live happily, successfully, prosperously. Didn't He say, "I came that ye may have life, and may have it abundantly"? In other words, He taught not merely a way to be good and moral and honest and industrious and all that, but a way to live by the law that brings success and money and fame and love and all the other things that we want. And the law He taught was give—and give first—if you want to get anything. He voiced the Golden Rule "Whatsoever ye would that men should do to you, do ye even so to them." The wisest of the world's cynics say that you have to pay sometime for whatever you get. Jesus of Nazareth says, practically, "Pay as you enter." Select what you want, and pay first.

Maybe this sounds impracticable to you. It did to me. But try it out. I did. You'll get results. I did. It won't fail you. It hasn't failed me. Why? Because there is just one maker of law in the universe and that is the power we call

God, and that power made the law of giving and receiving. Give the best you have and look for the best in return. God challenges you and me to prove the promises He makes in the Bible, and these promises are simply statements of law that never fail of fulfillment. "Prove me now," says God, "whether I will not open the windows of heaven and pour you out a blessing greater than ye are able to receive." His only condition is that we shall "give first"—that's all. Commonly we do not take this sort of promise seriously; but it is sound and true. Is there anything wrong about the foregoing argument? God *is* the law. He is the law of love, which is only another name for the law of giving and receiving. If you will stop thinking of God as a joke, or as a terror, or as a myth, or as a dream, or as something far off and outside everyday life, and will think of Him as the Maker of the law of gravitation and of the law of love, one of which is just as real as the other—you'll get somewhere.

If you want to know how, the whole secret lies in beginning. The way to do it is to do it. Right where you are, now, begin to give something good to the person nearest to you, and keep on doing it, no matter what you seem to get back at first. *Do!* Don't talk! And you'll lift yourself out of your troubles, no matter what they seem to be or how deeply you seem to be sunk in them. Try it. You'll be surprised. I was. Try it as patiently and as hard as you would try to get a drink of water if you were very thirsty. You'll get a return, a reward, that you don't even dream of yet. You *will!* Don't let anybody fool you about it.

And besides, if it doesn't work, you don't have to keep on with it. But you will keep on—if you give it a fair chance to prove itself. Because—it works.

WORKING WITH GOD

Any Job You Want

YOU CAN have any job you want. You do not believe that, do you? That is why you do not get the job you want now; you do not believe you can get it. Did you ever hear Mark Twain's advice to the young seeker after a job? He said something like this: "Pick out the man you want to work for, and then go and work for him. Tell him you are going to work for him for nothing till he decides you are worth something, and how much." That seems an absurd piece of advice. But it will certainly work if you really put it into practice. Now, think a moment with me.

If you get a job—any sort of a job—what will your employer pay you for? For the work you do, of course. Will he pay you in advance? He will not. He will pay you after you have worked a month, a week, a day. How much will he pay you? What you earn, of course. Will he pay you more than you are worth—even if he has agreed to? He will not. If you do not measure up to specifications, he will get out of his agreement in one way or another. He will discharge you, or if he has made a contract with you, he will break it or make you break it, or make your situation intolerable, or buy you off. He will certainly not pay you for something you do not give him.

Here is that saying in the business world again,

that you cannot get something for nothing. You cannot. This means that you cannot get salary or wages for something you do not do. Do you think you see men getting paid for something they are not delivering? Watch them. Watch the loafers and the quitters and the "soldiers."

But there is a deeper thing under this fact and these appearances than people commonly think. It is this: Justice! Justice does work in the affairs of men, whether they recognize it or not. You do not believe it? Study it. Men do get what they want—what they really want. You can get what you really want, as we have said—and you will get it, whether you know it or not!

"But," you say, "just as good men have failed of their aim as have succeeded." So? What does it mean to be "good"? Goodness, in the ordinary sense, has nothing to do with the matter. If it had, we could not understand the situation at all. People who try to explain success or failure on the ground of goodness never do understand it—nor anything else they try to explain on the same ground. Because "goodness" or "badness" in the ordinary moral sense is not the reason. Law is the reason, for everything.

"Whatsoever ye shall ask in prayer, believing, ye shall receive." Real virtue consists in keeping in harmony with the law—or trying to. Goodness, in this sense, is always rewarded, and badness, in the same sense, is always punished. That is, the law works for those who keep it and works against those who choose to go against it. I do not dare to set any limits. I do not believe there are any limits. It does not make the least difference in the world whether we know the law or not—it works. "Ignorance of the law is no excuse." And you cannot blame some far-off God for your actions, or for anything that happens to you, or for your knowing the law or not knowing it. It is up to you!

Does that frighten you? Or if you believed it, would it frighten you? Instead of frightening you it should encourage you, inspirit you, stir you up to your highest ambition, fill you with your highest hope, assure you of realization of your highest desire, make you certain of success, and happy beyond your dreams! Because you cannot lose!

Now, let us see. We have made some pretty rash statements, have we not? From the ordinary, unbelieving standpoint, yes. But it is not bumptiousness to state law, nor modesty to understate it. What have we said? You can have anything you really want. Well, you can; the thing you want is among the possibilities for you or you would not want it. Desire is implanted in you by a power that intends you to have what that desire calls for. You have no desires that this power has not given you. Desire was meant to be fulfilled—consuming, supreme desire, not the piddling little wishes that do not even last over night or past mealtime. Your real desire becomes the great purpose of your life; and it matters not what that purpose is, you are going to get a reward commensurate with your single-heartedness. Remember, your desire is implanted in you by this power we are talking about.

This power will grant the desire—has already granted it—because this power is the only power there is in the universe. It is the power for which another name is God. He is the only power you will ever know, and the only power you will ever get a job from; the only power you will ever work for and the only power that will ever pay you. You may think you ask some man or woman for a job, but you do not really. You "ask" the universal law for that job. And because the universal law (God) has put the desire for that job in you, you will get it. And because that same universal law is the paymaster you will get paid for it, and no man or woman on earth can prevent it. You are working for God, not man. God is the one to whom you go for your job, for whom you labor, from whom you receive your reward. You cannot help it; that is the way it is. It is so, whether you believe it or not, whether you know it or not, whether you like it or not!

But you remind me that I have said that all desire comes from God. It may be well enough to think that the desire to work comes from the one power, but does the desire of the thief to steal come also from the Supreme Being? To steal, no. To possess, yes. Every instinct, appetite and aspiration is implanted in man by God. But who is God? Why, God is my Creator. God is my life, my strength, my intelligence, my mind. Now turn the statement around. My being is God, my life is God, my intelligence is God, my mind is God. Do you pretend to say that you have a desire independent of your mind? Hardly. Well, that is the answer.

The answer is that God, instead of being something outside of you, is within you, controlling all your affairs through you. Is it hard to believe that you have only to realize that overwhelming conception in order to have God come forth visibly into your affairs, whatever they are, whoever you are, wherever you are, whatever your circumstances appear to be? You are an individual expression of God. You create what you choose. How? First by thinking it. That is the only way anything is created—by thought. If you think that things are created by hammer and nails, or steam shovels, or dynamos, or lathes, or trowels, or giant powder, or printing presses, or congresses, or kings, you have never thought even so far back as the drafting table or the blue pencil!

Things are created by thought in the mind, and by nothing else and nowhere else. Yes, by your thought, and in your mind. And when you begin to realize that, you will begin to work for the God who is universal Mind, in you and in me and in everybody else, and in everything in the universe. You will realize that you cannot fail to do what you really want to do and have what you really want to have.

How shall you begin? By going after that first job with an idea in your mind just the reverse of what you have been trying to hold there. Think not about what you are going to get, but about what you can give. Ask for opportunity to give, and give with all your heart all you have got, knowing that you cannot fail to get what your desire calls for. You cannot fail to get back what you give out. For who are you? You are the expression of God in your individuality. Think of that. In Him you live and move and have your being. You are one with God, the supreme power in the universe. You are one with supreme universal Mind. And universal Mind creates what it wants to create. In other words, it gives out what it wants to see manifested. Think of it. Think! You! Not somebody else—you! You cannot fail!

Obedience to Law

WHAT IS OBEDIENCE to law in everyday practice? Let us study it in its opposite. Let us consider one of the commonest of everyday failures to obey law. When somebody who does not know as much about it as you do says you are wrong; when somebody "knocks" you behind your back; when somebody slyly undermines your standing with the boss; when somebody takes advantage of your kindness, cheats you, robs you, strikes you—why, it is easy to get mad! And yet even a prize fighter knows enough not to get mad. He knows that it is the worst method in the world by which to accomplish the purpose he has in view.

It is the worst method to use to accomplish any purpose whatever. Let us see what it usually accomplishes. I know a man who gets mad when somebody tries to steal the right of way from him when he is driving his car. The other night a man rushed past him, cut in short ahead of him and crowded him out of his rightful place in the traffic. My friend "got mad." When the traffic opened so that he could, he speeded up, caught up with the other fellow, rushed past him, and cut in short ahead of him in retaliation, in a "how-do-you-like-it-yourself" spirit. What happened? He turned a little too short, caught the other fellow's front fender, and crumpled his own nice new rear fender most annoyingly—and expensively. And then he noticed that the other car was a ragged old flivver that could not be damaged much by anything that could be done to it. And he discovered that he had just put a bad mark on his own car as a "reward" for yielding to temper, for pampering his tendency to temper! Also he knew that he had narrowly escaped worse, for that sort of thing is playing with disaster, as we can always see plainly enough afterwards.

When a man gets mad he befogs his judgment. Virtually always he does something foolish, sometimes he does things that seem insane, sometimes he does irretrievable things, tragic, fatal things! What he does always ranges somewhere between silliness and crime. The young man or girl who "talks back" to an employer, the teacher or parent or man or woman who gives rein to white hot passion and says scathing, lacerating, cruel things or deals blows with a fist or a weapon, simply surrenders to an emotion and lets it run his life— usually to the point of shame, sometimes to the point of disgrace, and sometimes—once too often —to murder! That's the way murders are done— letting passion rule instead of intelligence!

But the worst of it all does not lie in the deed you do when you get mad. It lies in yielding the management of your life to emotion or passion instead of intelligence. I once heard a fine lecture by Norman Angell, a man who thinks so clearly that it has made him famous, in which he said something like this: "Most of the troubles in the world are caused by the fact that men act under the sway of passion rather than of intelligence. Every sort of disagreement, from private quarrel to world-wide war, comes from this tragic vice of men."

You know history well enough to trace the truth of this. And you can find in the newspapers every day stories enough of the police court and the divorce court and the criminal court to illustrate it amply. And you know your own life well enough to see a dozen examples of it. You can recall a score of cases in which men let go of intelligence and grasped madness when they "got mad"!

And it is always disastrous. Why? Because "love . . . is the fulfillment of the law." And we are living in a universe where law reigns supreme, simple, quiet, unalterable, undeviating, terrible, beneficent law! Law makes the world go round, and runs the stars quietly, changelessly, beautifully, terribly, gloriously. Law makes your blood circulate and your perspiration flow; makes the ball bound and the volcano erupt; makes the violet bloom and the tide sweep; makes the fire burn and the blizzard freeze; makes the frog leap and the whale spout; makes the thunder startle and the sunshine delight; makes violence destroy and thought create!

Law! Everywhere law! And everywhere good law. Every law you know is a good law. Every law of nature, so-called, works for your good and mine the moment we obey it. There is no such thing as a bad law. What? You ask if it is not a bad law that makes fire burn me when I touch it? No. It's a good law misused. All law is good law. All law is part of one law, and that one law is the law of good. Sometimes it is called the law of love. But what does love mean? It means good will, that's all. You will good to the one you love. You cannot express the idea of love any better than that if you try for years.

But then——! Why, if the law of good, the law of love, is the one great law that includes all law, I can see why it is foolish to get mad. I can see why it is madness to get mad. It is going contrary to all law. No matter what my so-called provocation may be, it is just plain insanity to get mad. Why, it is ridiculous to get mad just because somebody else does, to defy the law just because somebody else does. It is just like putting one's hand on a hot stove because somebody else does. If I am up in an airplane and another passenger jumps out, I should be a plain imbecile if I jumped out too just to prove to him that he is wrong, to force him to admit that he is wrong, to convince him that he is a fool—on the way down.

We may as well make up our mind that we cannot break law. It does not break. If I try to break it, it breaks me. Getting mad is just as bad as jumping out of an airplane, and its results are just as inevitable. It always makes either a fool or a criminal of me.

Now, how did this man Jesus, of whom we

Obedience to Law

hear so much, put it? Why, He saw so plainly the utter folly of getting mad that He said in effect, "Go to the other extreme. Turn the other cheek! Love your enemies! Do good to the chap that tries to injure you! Suppose he does try to injure you and that you do do good to him, it is he that is disobeying the law, not you. He is the fellow that is jumping out of the airplane, not you. He is the one that will suffer, not you."

I often wonder why we get sentimental over the teachings of Jesus when they are just so much horse sense, yes, thoroughbred horse sense. Do you know, just between you and me, the more I think about the things that this man Jesus of Nazareth said, the deeper grows my respect for Him. Do you know, I used to think that He was an impractical sentimentalist Himself. Then I began to see that some of the things He taught were sound common sense, and I felt like taking my hat off to Him. Now, as I watch the law of love at work in the universe and in my world right here and now, transforming life for me at every touch, and as I remember that this Jesus of Nazareth spent His life and gave His life and took up His life again, all to prove to me that the law of love is the one law and that it works now and here and always, perfectly, why, I want to go on my knees to Him!

WORKING WITH GOD

Keeping the Whole Law

GOD'S WORK is done. He is the law. He is the supply. Our work is to obey the law, to receive and distribute the supply. One of the things to which we seem most persistently blind when we first begin to apply Truth principles is that we must take the initiative: We must begin obeying the law before it begins working for us. We've mentioned this. But let us repeat: We must turn on the electricity before we get light. We must walk out into the sunshine before we feel its warmth. We must put the weight on the scales before the balance tips. We must light the fuse before the blast goes off. We must snap the shutter of the camera before we get a picture. We must strike the key before the organ tone responds.

In many cases the response is instantaneous; in others it requires time. If we would grow potatoes we must plant them and wait for them to grow. If we would hatch chickens, we must put the eggs under the hen or in the incubator, and wait through the incubating period. If we would make bread, we must put it into the oven and wait until it is baked. All this is as we see it from our present standpoint.

The most easily recognizable differences between everyday work and what we commonly call miracles are two. One has to do with the part that we suppose we play in initiating causes, and the other has to do with the lapse of time that we believe necessary between the causes and their effects. The more we learn about the laws that govern the doing of anything, the less we see ourselves as initiating agents, and the more the time lapse shrinks.

We previously classified as a miracle the instantaneous occurrence of an event that we have been accustomed to seeing occur slowly. But we cease to call things miracles when we see them as consistent results of the operation of laws, even when we bring the time lapse down to the fraction of a second.

Let us go a step further with this idea. Electric light, as now apparently "produced" by the touching of a button, would have been a miracle in the days before men learned the laws back of the phenomenon. A hundred years ago it took perhaps a month to send a message across the Atlantic; today a man speaks in London and is simultaneously heard in New York. Miracle? Not at all; radio.

It is difficult to understand how any one even vaguely familiar with the scientific progress of the last fifty years can doubt the possibility of so-called miracles, or question, on the ground of impossibility, the miracles of Jesus of Nazareth. Whether the historical accounts that we have of Jesus' miracles are correct to the last detail or not is beside the point. One can hardly look at what is today commonly done, and say that Jesus' miracles, as described, were impossible.

But the results of obedience to law, whether swift or slow, are sure; that point any sane student will admit. It follows as a corollary that the way to test any alleged statement of law, to learn whether or not it does truly state law, is to try it; for law must work if its conditions are fulfilled. Law is not a person with powers of choice; law has no choice but to obey its own terms. So, in considering the work that we have to do, let us consider the statements of law by authorities that we have some reason to respect, and recognize that putting them to the test must necessarily be a part of the task. Jesus, the master of obedience to law and consequently the master of its results, gave a few statements of law for us to test. He suggested that we test them. He begged us to test them. It was the chief purpose of His life and death to induce us to test and prove them. He lived and died with the one great purpose of demonstrating that testing them proves them. He proved them. He used them, and for Him they overcame the world.

What were these rules? "Thou shalt love the Lord thy God with all thy heart, and with all thy soul, and with all thy mind" and "Thou shalt love thy neighbor as thyself." And He gave admonitions such as these: Turn the other cheek. Give your cloak with your coat. Go the second mile. Did it ever occur to you that it may be called a discovery of Jesus' that, if it is good to follow a principle a little way, it is well to go further; in the parlance of the street, to "go the limit" on it? That, in substance, is what Jesus begs us to do. Paraphrased, His instructions might read: "Fear not; only go all the way in your observance of law." If His instructions express law, that law will work once or a million times. If it is law it will work in New York or Honolulu, Japan or Kamchatka, the earth or Mars, now, tomorrow, and throughout eternity. And Jesus says that love is law.

How simple it all is! Here in black and white are twenty-eight words, on which Jesus said "the whole law hangeth, and the prophets." We have only to follow their instructions just as they are written, in order to test that statement of His. If the benefits of being in harmony with law accrue to us, instantly or gradually, we may fairly conclude that He spoke the truth. Until we do test them and find them untrue, we can hardly say that what He said cannot be true, or that it is thoroughly impracticable in modern life. Can we?

If one who is a pianist opens a new piece of music, he finds certain marks and signs called notes set down there in black and white. If he follows them, striking indicated keys on his instrument in certain time, he will find that he has fulfilled a law that produces harmony, and music will be the concrete result. If a person is a mathematician and he finds a certain rule set down in black and white in a work on mathematics, he tries it and gets the promised result. If he is a gardener and follows the black-and-white instructions for planting and cultivating that are printed on any package of seeds, he gets flowers or vegetables from those seeds. If he reads the black-and-white instructions for running his new car and follows them, he will run the car.

But we must do all that the rules require. We must go the limit. We cannot make music by striking notes a half tone off those set down in the score; we cannot get four by adding two and one and nine tenths; we cannot get morning-glories by putting the seeds into the ground and refusing to cover them or to water them; we cannot run a car by merely opening the throttle, while we refuse to shift the gears. In short, we must obey the law, the whole law, and nothing but the law, if we would have its good results.

Oh, yes, one may give a partial obedience—and get an indifferent result. That is what most of us do. And sometimes seemingly slight departures from the law in one respect are the obscure causes of failure in seemingly unrelated respects. Have you ever applied this idea to some condition in your finances or in your bodily health that has seemed mysterious to you, and have you carefully scanned your daily conduct to find the departure from law that was the obscure cause? It is an accepted belief that anger, indulged in, will stop the processes of digestion. Will gossip, indulged in, affect the size of my income? Will white lying, indulged in, load my muscles with fatigue? It is not until we take off all the limits

Keeping the Whole Law

and go all the way in keeping the law that we get —miracles!

A thousandth-of-an-inch variation from specifications in the machining of an engine shaft will produce friction enough in its bearings to ruin them. A hundredth-of-an-inch error in the line of lip or eyelid will ruin a portrait. Why can we not see the obvious parallel and use plain common sense in following exactly, completely, undeviatingly such a law as that of love—the great fundamental law containing all other law? "Love therefore is the fulfillment of the law," said Paul.

"Ye therefore shall be perfect" seems a hard saying. But why so? We hold the standard of perfection in obedience to natural law. We must. Why not accept the same standard of obedience to spiritual law? Besides, what is more natural than spiritual law, which underlies natural law as spiritual substance underlies visible phenomena?

Natural laws as we know them fit together in a perfect and continuous order. A thousand analogies indicate the same harmony and continuity among spiritual laws. Harmony is the *sine qua non* of the universe; without it we could not exist. The law of love is the law of harmony. Yet people will tell you that living by the law of love is not practical. It is not—if you go only part way. The way to obey is to obey—completely.

No man is honest who is only partly honest; no statement is true that is only partly true; no signature is valid that is only nine tenths written; no water is ice that is only near-frozen; no stone is over the hill that lacks an inch of the crest; no stock is at par that is one point below; no ship is in port that is just outside; no cistern is tight that has just a little crack in it; no man is alive who is just a little dead! You keep no law till you go all the way. No result is achieved that is just barely missed. A miss is as good as a mile.

But why miss? Learning not to miss is what we have to do, isn't it?

Pure Christianity, that is, the Christianity that Jesus of Nazareth Himself taught, seems to me highly practical.

I am a business man. My problems are real to me. My primary reason for turning to practical Christianity is to find solutions for my problems; *my* problems.

They are instant to me, these problems, immediate, pressing. I have employees to pay, a family to support, food, clothing, shelter to provide. I am thinking of these problems almost constantly. Whatever else I may be doing, wherever I may be, I think of them more or less continually. I must, since it is my job to provide the things that are necessary to my business and to my family. Will practical Christianity help me in this? Is practical Christianity "practical"?

Let us consider a little further. Perhaps we shall see whether it is practical or not.

Here is a formula for concrete: cement, sand, water. It is a formula that has been tried and proved. I have decided that I will follow it. I put in the sand and the water. Shall I put in the

Keeping the Whole Law

cement? How much shall I put in? Can I do with less? Shall I skimp a bit? What will happen if I do? But this is a formula, tried and proved, meant to be followed. How far shall I go?

Here is a standard of weights and measures. It says that sixteen ounces make a pound. Are there sixteen ounces in the pound I buy? Are there sixteen ounces in the pound I sell? I have a standard. Shall I live up to it, or shall I skimp a little? What will happen if I subtract an ounce from each pound? How far shall I go?

I am sending a special delivery letter, which calls for ten cents postage. If I put on but nine cents, what will happen? Can't I skimp a little? But here is a standard—a law, in fact—that calls for ten cents. Shall I obey?

My business is music. I have here a composition I desire to play. Here is the theme in a dozen bars. Shall I play eleven? Can't I skimp a little? But the theme is the foundation of the composition. What will happen if I cut it short? How far shall I go?

Questions like these can be multiplied indefinitely. What are they all about? They are about formulas for doing things well. The problem is whether or not, when such formulas have been tried and proved, they should be followed exactly, completely, in order to produce desired results; or whether, when they have been tried and proved, they are to be discarded, tampered with, followed only part way.

You wonder how a sane man can ask such

questions. You consider it falling short of your standard of sanity even to consider dropping items out of formulas that have been tried and proved. Yes, it is unnecessary for these questions to be answered audibly, or in writing. They can be answered in your heart of hearts.

We are after results. Can we get perfect results or hope to get them, anywhere, if we are unwilling to fulfill the conditions laid down in the formula? Can we get perfect results by giving short measure? Oh, yes, perhaps we can "get away with it" for a while. But if I cut short the formula, or the measure, is there any question—is there ever any question—of the ultimate result?

Suppose I take a chance, as I sometimes do with the speed laws. What then? Suppose I take a chance and give short measures? Let us pause to ask a pointed question about my procedure: Do I advertise short measures? No. Well, why not? Because I expect to fool somebody by means of my short measure. I expect that somebody is going to take it for full measure, and therefore pay me for full measure; and therefore I shall make a profit, a little more profit, a little more immediate profit. How interesting and enticing! Profit is the legitimate purpose of my business, isn't it?

But whom do I expect to fool? Do I fool the oven with a short-measure recipe? Do I fool the sun and frost and earthquake with short-measure concrete? Do I fool the laws of harmony when I play false notes? Do I fool the laws of force when I take a chance with the rules of the road? Whom and what do I expect to fool when I take a chance? Myself?

Of what do I take a chance? Disaster, nothing less. And I not only take a chance, I not only invite; I make sure of disaster.

Now here is that formula for practical Christianity about which I have asked. Is it practical? It is offered to me as a formula for life. How far shall I go?

"Thou shalt love the Lord thy God with all thy heart, and with all thy soul, and with all thy strength, and with all thy mind; and thy neighbor as thyself." Put a pencil mark under that repeated little word "all" and under that other little one-syllable word "as." That is all you need do to make the whole point of all this clear. Here is your formula, in black and white, unmistakable, tried, and proved, and set down to be followed: the standard in the business of living. A formula for life, just as exact and as scientific as any other. Indeed, it is far more vital than any other, because it is all-inclusive. In its strict observance it holds all the conditions of success in anything.

Do we think we can skimp it?

Remember that Jesus even elaborated on it, in order to tell us how far we must go. He told us that it means, "Love your enemies and do good to those who despitefully use you." Hard sayings? Why? Isn't all this perfectly consistent with the general rule about formulas? Are not formulas based on law, and are they not meant to be kept? Are they not meant to get results?

And what are the results that we are promised? Well, suppose we turn back to the Old Testament and see what God says about it; this God whom we recognize as the maker of law: the law of concrete, of music, of love—this God who is Himself the law. Ah, yes, He said something to the effect that we are to bring all the tithes into the storehouse and prove Him now herewith, if He will not open to us the windows of heaven and pour us out a blessing greater than we are able to receive. Rather a generous promise, is it not? A generous fulfillment, rather; a fulfillment of conditions to be established by me; of conditions laid down in our formula for living.

Do I expect to get results? Where do I skimp? Is practical Christianity practical? I am told by those who have tried it, from men who work beside me and have tried it out here, all the way back through history to Jesus Christ Himself, who proved it to the ultimate limit, that it is a formula that works. I am promised that it will work to my everlasting good. Shall I observe it in the same generous, unlimited, complete way in which I want it to work for me? If I do not, whom do I expect to fool? With what am I taking a chance? How far shall I go?

Learning to Love

YOU HAVE HEARD people say, "I don't know what it means to love God. How can I love Him, when I don't know Him?" Maybe you've said that yourself. I have.

But Jesus Christ said, "He that hath my commandments, and keepeth them, he it is that loveth me." Does this mean that obedience is love? or does it mean that obedience is the evidence of love? or does it mean that obedience is the road to love? Does it matter which it means? "If any man will do his will, he shall know of the doctrine."

What did Jesus Himself do? He "went about doing good." He knew how to love God. Did you ever wonder what His early life must have been, before He began His ministry? I wonder if perhaps He did not spend all that first thirty years of His life learning how to love God by keeping His commandments; and how to love His neighbors by serving them. It seems to me that that must have been what He did, and that that is the explanation of all His wonderful power to help and heal and serve—and love. Just think of that young Jewish boy, whom the world called Jesus, son of Joseph and Mary, going quietly about "doing good" all through His youth and young manhood, and learning that it was the secret of power. Think of thirty years spent just learning the marvelous results of simply doing good. What a love developed in Him!

Don't you think love would develop in you and in me, if we made it our whole business to serve the good—which is God—and our neighbors? Psychologists say that when we do another person a favor we become interested in him as if we had an investment in him. The more we do for him the more interested we are in him. If we do much, we come to love him. Maybe one of the explanations of the love of mothers for their children is that mothers do so much for their children.

We do not love our friends for what they do for us. Most of us would readily admit that the joy of love is in giving. "It is more blessed to give than to receive." I wonder if that's not because the blessing of the giver is that he grows to know what love is, what it means to him, the lover. What experience have you ever had in loving? Did you get your greatest happiness in that love out of what the loved one did for you? Was your greatest joy in the fact that that loved one loved you? Or was your happiness—your joy—in loving, and expressing it by every means you could find?

One of the magazines some years ago published a story about a young man who went to work in the foreign correspondence department of a mercantile house in New York. He had very little experience, but he was full of enthusiasms. He was full of wants and desires.

It happened that the firm had tried for years to get the business of a great manufacturer of Panama hats in a certain South American country. But no salesman or buyer for the American house had ever been able to get an order or a bill of goods from the Panama hatters. Some reason kept the foreign firm from doing business with the New York concern.

But our young man—let's call him Smart—wanted a Panama hat. He thought maybe he could get one—a fine one that would otherwise be beyond his modest means at home—by asking the manufacturers in the southern clime to send him one. So he sat himself down and wrote a letter asking the head of the Panama hatters to send him a fine Panama—at a price he could afford to pay. And strangely enough, the foreign hatter, seeing an opportunity to do the New York importer a favor, seized upon it. He got the hat for young Smart and sent it to him with his compliments.

But the queer part of it was the sequel. After the hat was received young Smart followed up by asking Mr. Panama Hatter for a share of his business for the New York house. And Mr. P. H. found himself so interested in young Smart, and in the firm he worked for, because Mr. P. H. had done him a favor, that he listened to reason—with the result that he became persuaded to enter upon regular business relations. To the amazement of his employers, young Smart got the Panama hatters' business—after everybody else had failed.

Humorously that illustrates the principle involved. A recent book called "Strategy in Handling People" tells many similar stories and presents the same principle. If you want anybody to like you or favor you, get him to do you a favor. And if it works that way, it will work the other way too. If you want to be interested in somebody else, or to love him, do something for him.

What a light that sheds on human relations! How many divorces do you suppose would be prevented, if people just knew that principle and acted upon it. Yet the teaching of Jesus on that single point antedated modern psychology and modern strategy in handling people by some nineteen hundred years.

It is strange, when you stop to think of it, how all the theories and maxims and rules point back to the same basic principle. The way to receive what we want is to give to others what we should want them to give us. The way to love is to give. Give service. Did you ever know a servant who did not like the master or mistress whom he served faithfully? Did you ever know an employee who did not speak well of an employer to whom he was giving real, faithful service? Did you ever work for anybody you did not like, and give him full service without coming to like him?

You know, we are quite helpless against this law—because it is a law. We cannot help loving where we serve. If it is our country, or our city, or our club, or our lodge, or our church; if we are real workers in behalf of any organization,

Learning to Love

we shall love it. Unless we *are* workers, our affection will be cool at the best.

Did you ever keep a garden, or bees, or chickens, or cattle, or horses, or teach school, or wait on customers, or serve in any capacity where your labor contributed directly to the welfare of animals or men or children? If you have, nobody can tell you anything about this principle. You cannot help knowing it if your work was faithfully done. You could not help loving if your service was true and loyal and devoted.

If there is anybody that you feel you should love and that you find it hard not to hate, try doing something for him—something real, such as you would want somebody else to do for you. It works wonders in you! What causes your feeling of dislike, or anger, or hatred toward another person? Isn't it more often than not a consciousness of having injured him? Is there any surer way to hatred than to do another an injury? Isn't that axiomatic, and isn't it good psychology too?

If I find that I do not love God—the good—I'd better look out. It simply means I am not serving Him. Perhaps it means that I am trying to oppose Him, disobeying His commandments, injuring some of His children, working against the kingdom. And if I find that I am coming to love God, the good; what does it mean? Shouldn't it be a source of great reassurance that the good is really dear to me? But then, if it is, nobody has to tell me the reason. I know, or at any rate I have a working principle that fills me with satisfaction and happiness.

Like all great principles it works both ways. Serving gives birth to loving; and loving to serving. It sets up what we call a benign circle—blessing piled upon blessing, good reacting in good, joy reacting in happiness.

"Bless them that curse you, pray for them that despitefully use you." Why? Because it will make me love them. But why should I love them? Because that is the commandment of the God whom I want to learn to love.

Love is its own reward. Nobody who does not love knows anything about love. But we do not have to be ignorant—the way is plain. The way to the greatest joy that ever was conceived—loving the God who *is* love and who so constituted human hearts that they take fire with happiness at the only true communion with Him that is possible—the love of the heart for divine love.

WORKING WITH GOD

Open Channel

DO YOU SUPPOSE anything can interfere with the flow of good from God to you?

Do you think anything is interfering with that flow? Do you wish you might receive more of some good than you are receiving? Are you free from disappointments and discouragements?

Could your child—your boy or girl—refuse to receive a gift that you wished to give to him or to her? Or could that child do something that would seriously interfere with your giving that gift? Not because you would cease to want to give, but because the child's action would make the giving difficult?

What would it most likely be that would make giving a gift to your child difficult for you? Would it be some form of ingratitude on his part, some disobedience, some disrespect, some rebellion? Would it make you hesitate in giving, if you should see your boy or girl do something unkind or cruel to somebody else? If you should see in your son a persistent inclination to injure other people, would your impulse to give him the things you knew he wanted be just as compelling as ever? Suppose you had specially told him that the one thing you wanted him to do was to show good will to neighbors, friends, business acquaintances, strangers; and suppose he regularly showed them unkindness, and dealt them injury behind their backs?

Of course, your boy or girl never does such things. But do you know anybody's child who does? Does such conduct seem to you a good reason why the child's parent should hesitate about granting his son or daughter special favors, special gifts, satisfying his or her heart's desires, granting his or her urgent requests?

Suppose the child who asked and did not receive the favor or the gift from his father that he greatly wanted should try to learn why. Do you suppose it would ever occur to him to think that his own conduct had anything to do with it? Do you suppose he might suspect that, though his father certainly loved him well, and though his father provided regularly for most of his wants, and though his father gave him constantly many things that he needed and wanted, still it might be just possible that he, the son, made it hard for the father to give him the special gifts, the great things, the marked favors, the "heart's desires" because of deliberate disobedience to and disregard of the father's special requests?

Well, if I am not getting from my heavenly Father just what I want most to get, does it ever occur to me that I may not be doing the things He specially asks me to do? What does He ask me to do? Why, to show good will to neighbors and acquaintances and strangers—doesn't He? Well, do I show good will?

Oh yes, I am polite to other people. I show them ordinary courtesies. I even do favors sometimes for people to whom I think I owe nothing. I do quite a lot of creditable things when I am in their company—to their faces. But what do I do in their absence—behind their backs? Do I show them good will then? Am I the kind that is a friend to a man's face, and an enemy behind his back? That is, do I show him a face of good will, and then knife him from behind? Do I give attention to his bodily ease and his pleasure in company, and then stab him in the reputation when he isn't looking? Do I salve him with flattery when he is in a position to defend himself, and then set the fire of ridicule going among his friends when he is off guard?

Do I, for instance, lead the applause at the luncheon or the club meeting, where Bill Johnson speaks, and slap him on the back afterwards and tell him it was great—and then whisper to Smith on the way out, "Well, old Bill was just as great a bore as usual. I wonder if his wife never tells him to get some new stories?"

Do I, for instance, congratulate Jim Smith on his promotion to the place of general manager—and then tell Tom Warren, "Yes, Smith got the job all right, but he won't last long. He's a slave driver."

Do I, for instance, talk public-spiritedly about standing shoulder to shoulder in time of business stress, and then tell Ken Travis that Tom Warren will bear watching and that "he is sure to trim you if you are not careful."

Do I, for instance, comment with a grin on Jessup's frayed tie, or Halley's grammatical break, or high words I overheard between Sanders and his wife, or the grass that grows up through Hemming's front walk, or Brown's pallid paunchiness, or Lane's rotten old pipe, or Barnes's impudent children, or Perry's long fish story, or Bell's embarrassment when called on to speak at the church supper? Do I go around making good stories out of the failings of other people, getting laughs at their expense, cutting their reputations to ribbons, scorching their friendships to raise a laugh? Do I?

Well, my Father particularly asked me not to do that sort of thing, didn't He? Didn't He say, first, through my Elder Brother, "Judge not"? Then didn't He say, "Love one another," and "whatsoever ye would that men should do unto you . . ."? Didn't He? Well, just why do I disobey and disregard His special requests? Do I expect that it is going to make it easier for Him to give me mine?

Basil King, in his remarkable book "Faith and Success," tells of an almost miraculous change in his fortunes, when he stopped doing little unkindnesses behind people's backs. It was a singularly honest and singularly helpful confession. He said he came to the conclusion that the channel between him and God—or rather between God and him—was like other channels, more often filled up with silt than with great falls of rock, and that the silt that fills up the God channel is made up of what we think of as "little" sins—little meannesses, little bits of unkind ridicule, little bits of gossip, little unfavorable comments, little offenses against the law of love, while "great" sins like stealing and killing are rare among us. But "silt"—a lot of it, gathering by slow accretion—may fill up the channel just as effectively as a great fall of rock! Maybe a lot more effectively.

But who says that the propagation of scandal or the promotion of ridicule is a little thing? One is stealing a man's reputation; the other is killing other people's respect for him! Can I be continually guilty of that kind of stealing and killing and hope that God can find it easy to give me the things my heart cries out to Him for?

Do I not brand myself as an arrant coward when I talk unkindly behind another's back, saying things unfavorable, whether true or not? Am I not that most despicable of creatures, the snake in the grass? Am I not that most cruel of enemies, the one who injures another unwarned and unaware? Is there any excuse for me? What do you think of me? Do I have to ask you if your opinion of me goes up, if your respect for me increases, when I bring you a discreditable story about somebody you and I know, or when I make a "funny crack" about some mutual acquaintance' misfortune or weakness? If you are a sound-thinking, decent-hearted citizen, you think less of me.

Well, is God a sound-thinking, decent-hearted citizen, or not? How do you suppose He looks at me?

Suppose you say, "But God is not a person, to be offended by my misdoings."

No, perhaps not—though God is everything that man is, isn't He? But suppose we say that God is law? Does that make it easier for me to adjust my meannesses, my unkindnesses, my cruelties, to His standards? If God is law, what is that law? Is it the law of love? If so, how can there be any harmony between His ways and mine, if mine are the ways of the snake in the grass? If there is a channel between Him and me, what is that channel for? What is supposed to flow through it? What do I want to flow through it? Good? Well, what chance has good to flow through that channel to me if I stuff it with dirt—the "dirt" I do to others behind their backs?

Maybe there is a revelation in this for you—as I think there was for Mr. King, by his own account. He tells his own story in the book I have mentioned. He says his "luck" changed the very day he stopped dealing in mean gossip and ridicule of others. He says that instead of having to go after the things he wanted, they began to come to him. He was blessed—so much blessed that he had to tell the world about it.

Sometimes we wonder why it is that we do not get the things we pray for, the heart's desires we cherish, even the good things, the generous, the unselfish things that we want for others only, not at all for ourselves. We can't understand why God withholds them, why He is so stingy with us, why He doesn't make good His word, why He doesn't "open . . . the windows of heaven, and pour" out what we want so much. Well, how can He? Maybe the channel is all clogged up with our "dirt"!

Remember, obscure causes are responsible for the results that we see in the world's affairs as in the body's health. "Little" things are more often than not the causes of the great evils. A sliver under the finger nail could spoil a great diplomat's effectiveness in debate; a corn could ruin a love affair; a blister might sap a hero's courage; a bad tooth might cause rheumatism in an ankle; too cold a shower on too warm a body might paralyze the spine; a snappish temper at the breakfast table can make a head ache all day —yours or somebody else's; continual pampering of an appetite can send a man under the surgeon's knife. Do you think it is a departure from the teachings of Truth to speak in such terms? Truth has to do with the operation of law, not with sentimental notions of poetic justice. "Whatsoever a man soweth, that shall he also reap." That is the law. That is the law of love!

Now, talking about a law, or a principle, or a method never got anybody anywhere. If I am not satisfied with what God is doing for me, here is a tip to follow. I can look into this channel of mine, and see what it is filled with. If I am convinced that the channel between God and me cannot be filled up by any means whatever—if I have that rash notion!—I can at least recognize that the channel of good will between other people and me can be filled up most quickly and most surely and most effectively by just the kind of silt we have been talking about. I said a little way back that you might hate me if you discovered me to be a backbiting gossip monger, whether the gossip was about yourself or about somebody else. Well, don't you suppose that your feeling toward me might interfere with the flow of some of God's good to me through you? Wouldn't a closed channel between you and me—closed by my meanness—have anything to do with God's supply to me? If not the channel between you and me, certainly the channel between some other human agent of God's distribution of good and me. For God distributes His good through human agents more often than not.

See what it comes to? Why it comes to this: The only way I can serve God is by serving my neighbors. Didn't Jesus say, "Inasmuch as ye have done *it* unto one of the least of these my brethren, ye have done *it* unto me"? God sends me most of my reward through my neighbors! You can be just as hard-boiled about it as you want to be, but you can't go back of the fact that the good will we get is sure to be proportioned sooner or later, right here on earth—in Kansas

City, or Chicago, or Seattle, or Boston, or Waterbury, or London, or Paris—to the good will we give out. So why not reckon with this element in life—reckon with the fact that great disappointments and frustrations may be due to obscure causes—little things like unkindnesses, white lies, bluffs, evasions, cowardly treacheries —betrayals of Truth! Let us reckon with this idea awhile, and see if results may not amaze us. Results of right action are always amazing!

Thinking about Thinking

Now, let's think about thinking. There is a popular superstition that the public does not want to think. Where it came from or who is sponsoring it would be hard to discover. But it is refuted and exploded before our eyes.

Everybody who has lived long enough to become aware of having any interest in anything finds pleasure in thinking. That he does not think about your pet subject or mine is no indication whatever that he does not think about his own pet subject or love to think about it.

You and I think about what we are interested in. It is the greatest pleasure we have. As often as not we do not realize it, we do not know the source of the pleasure we enjoy. We fancy that it is the easy chair, the satisfactory dinner, the comparative peace in the house after the children have gone to bed, or the opportunity to let go after "the strain of the day," thus soothing our nerves, relaxing our muscles, taking the burden off our brain. But it is not any one or all of these; it is the sheer satisfaction that always comes from letting loose the one great faculty that we possess.

We do the average person a great injustice in assuming that he does not think or that he does not want to think. Because he seems to take some

Thinking about Thinking

of his opinions ready-made from newspapers or from other people, why should we conclude that he has no ideas of his own? As a matter of fact, as soon as I fall in with this notion that he does not think, I am falling into the very shortcoming of which I am accusing him. And when I do that, I prove only one thing: that I am just like him, that I think clearly about some subjects and muddily about others. Why? Because I am interested in some subjects and not in others.

It is frequently said by people who profess to have studied the subject that thinking is an exceedingly difficult and unattractive job. We accuse average folks of dodging the task of thinking whenever they can. This charge is not true. If you and I do not choose to think about one subject, it is because we prefer to think about another. But think we do—and get out of it not merely most of our fun but all the fun we have.

You will probably grant that a boy is as natural a specimen of the human family as we can choose for an example. If your boy does not show any aptitude for study in school, you and his teachers are prompt to unite in declaring that he finds it hard and distasteful to think. But try him; give him something that vitally concerns him, and he will think—original thoughts.

Suppose your boy gets interested in a printing press, in building a radio receiving set, in collecting stamps, in devising football plays—in any pursuit that gives him a chance to think. He will think! He will think so hard and so earnestly and so feverishly that you can scarcely get him to go to bed at night; and he can scarcely sleep after he gets there. He will pore so steadily over catalogues, he will write so many letters, he will go so far out of his way to reach sources of information and supplies that he will give you concern for his health. He will spend his pocket money on his hobby, and he will work as you never saw him work before to get more for the purpose. He will desert the playground and go without his meals, if you will let him, to give his undivided attention to his pursuit.

Why? Right here is where we so often befool ourselves. We suppose that it is because he takes pride in some achievement, wants some result. But it is not that at all; for as soon as the thing is achieved, as soon as the result is accomplished, he drops it and cares little for it. And to your unintelligent despair and mine, he rushes off on a new tangent, after a fresh hobby. The reason is simple, as a boy's reasons always are. His whole pleasure in the first undertaking, and his whole pleasure in the subsequent ones that successively draw him away, lies in the thinking about them, and not in the mere possession of the result. Possession is nothing, says he!

Watch your little girl building or arranging her dolls' house. It is tremendous fun, absorbing every faculty just as long as it is in the doing. But when it is done, energy flags, concentration vanishes, busy hands drop, weariness appears. But let some one with a working imagination suggest a new use for the dolls' house, for entertaining doll guests, getting up a doll dinner, giving a doll party, and Little Daughter takes fire again and is not tired at all.

Why? Because all the fun was, and is, in the constructive thinking and not in the results! A past joy is of no more consequence than a past trouble. Retrospect is first cousin to stagnation —a saying worth thinking about.

All this has been said before? Certainly. But it is worth reiterating as long as the foolish statement is reiterated that people do not want to think, that they find it hard and distasteful to think, and that they will go to all lengths to avoid thinking. The answer to the reiterated lie must be the reiterated truth. And the reason for discussing it again is that thinking, being the most important thing in life as is admitted both by those who consider it fun and by those who do not—is worth thinking about, is really tremendously interesting to think about.

It may be that our psychologists believe, as they sometimes teach, that you cannot touch this subject without running into complications. But for the ordinary man there are no complications about it. To him thinking is as simple as eating, and more amusing.

Let us then consider a few examples among the adults. When a man has accumulated two dozen millions or so, we are accustomed to saying that he can enjoy only a small portion of them. We say that he keeps on accumulating not because

he wants the millions, but because he wants power.
As he gets power, we see him reach for more
power, and we say that he is insatiable. We do
not grasp the essential fact that primarily he
wants neither the millions nor the power, but the
joy of getting them that lies in the joy of creative
thought.

The woman who goes in for society has the
same motive and achieves the same result in kind.

But both the man and the woman become restless, dissatisfied, miserable, the moment the
achieving process comes to a pause in achievement.
Yet we call achievement success! It is nothing
of the kind; it is the achieving that is success—
for success is in finding happiness and in nothing
else. "If you miss the joy, you miss all!" All
achieving and all its fun lie in the thoughts that
precede and accompany it.

Football is an interesting sport, especially to
the players. But almost the moment a game is
won it ceases to be interesting. If this were not
so, the victories of last year would be more interesting than the defeats of this—and they are not.
If Yale loses to Harvard today, all details of the
game are first-page stuff in New Haven, Yale's
home, as well as in Harvard's home, Cambridge.
Nobody would think of filling a first page there
with details of last year's victory. Why? Because
the joy of football is in the game, and not in the
winning. If this were not true, it would be more
fun to have a team of supermen who could defeat
any rival in existence without effort than to have a

rival worthy in brawn and brain. Can you conceive anything duller in the world of sport than watching a game in which a superteam is playing? Such elimination of competition would kill sport!

As a bald proposition this is sometimes hard to see. But you have only to look carefully again at your own experience. That the pleasure in anything is in the process of doing it and not in the thing when it is done is as true as that the pleasure in riding continues only while the vehicle is moving. Men who think otherwise retire from active life when they suppose they have done the thing they wanted to do and have only to enjoy the wealth and the leisure they have earned. They become utterly wretched, they become nuisances to themselves and to everybody else, they develop diseases, if they do not get something else absorbing to think about. Without a vital interest, wealth and leisure will ruin any man.

Why? Because thinking is not only all the fun there is in life; it is all we live for—all of us!

Few things are more pitiable than the man who tries to get perpetual and satisfying joy out of past performances, even past triumphs. Men do not begin to live on reminiscences because they are growing old; they grow old because they begin to live on reminiscences. Give a man a topic about which to think, and he will not grow "prematurely old."

Often we mistake the thing that makes us happy. But is it ever far to seek? Isn't it always in the busy business of the mind? Can you imagine a heaven where there is no constructive thinking to do? Can you imagine a state where constructive thinking can go swimmingly on that will not be heaven?

Many years ago a boy lived in a little Oriental town. He grew up working at a common trade. He never made much money. He never held an office. He wrote no book and He invented no machine. He was neither doctor, lawyer, merchant, prince, nor soldier. In early maturity He was put to death for daring to think that certain popular superstitions were "bunk," and saying so. Yet it was He who put His home town on the map in letters so big that it is known the world over. As for His name, you would hesitate to put that of any other human being beside it as its equal in luster—and other persons have been writing books about Him ever since. And all because He made the discovery that the happiness and welfare of a man lie in his thinking. The moment His thesis is stated as He stated it, it won't be necessary to mention His name or that of His town. He said, "The kingdom of God is within you." "The kingdom of God," to most people who haven't been there, doubtless means, theoretically, that vague heaven of the future—the place where all happiness awaits us! But the very reason why we do not nowadays put people to death for thinking is that we are learning that He was right.

Yet we say that people do not like to think. One way of saying it is to assert that they want only to be amused. Theatrical producers make a slogan of the phrase "Give the public what it wants," and then try to eliminate from plays all material for audiences to think about. Motion pictures have been made upon the theory that they are necessarily for the "low-brow," because the low-brow predominates numerically in the world. The notion is that the low-brow is one who does not think. But if we adopt that definition, there is no such thing as a low-brow.

You disagree with this statement? And you find pleasure in disagreeing? Then it is because the assertion stirs you to think. It is not in the disagreement that you find pleasure—no; nor in your feeling of superiority to the propounder of the thesis. It is just because you are proving the thesis itself by getting fun out of thinking.

We have discussed together the popular superstition that thinking is hard work. The person who thinks so simply finds that the activity that does not tempt his eager thought is drudgery. Who is a bore? One who stirs in us no impulse to think. Why do we tire of reiteration? Because in it thought becomes static. Why do we rebel against creeds? Because they are simply the dead, finished results of yesterday's thinking, finalities in themselves, and have little to offer for today's fresh thought. Who is a dead man? One in whom thought has ceased—whether he is on his feet or under the sod. Who is a live man? One whose thoughts are afire. Who is the happy man? He who thinks.

Why came the cross-word puzzle? It is not

an entertainment for the moron alone; its fascination tempted the man and woman of brains. It stimulated thinking. Rudimentary? Perhaps; but all growing things begin that way. Why did bridge live and mah jong die? Why does Henry Ford say, with undoubted sincerity, that it would be fun to begin life over again? Why did Steinmetz hide himself away from fame and fortune in his laboratory, and why did Edison refuse to allow his hearing to be restored? All for the same reason: because it is fun to think—more fun to think than not to think—so much fun that men cast aside an occupation that rouses little thought for one that rouses more.

Anticipation is nine tenths of the joy of life, because anticipation is constructive thought. One who does not anticipate never enjoys anything. You say that an unexpected gift may give pleasure even when the surprise of it has allowed no opportunity for anticipation? It gives pleasure in exact proportion to the anticipation that it stirs as to the use of the gift. Give a woman a new car; she rejoices in anticipated riding—or parading. Give her the same car in a country without roads or spectators, and where is her pleasure in it? Elect a man to office; his satisfaction lies in his expectation of using it. Does applause please you and me? Only as it stirs us to build up in thought a further achievement. And he who learns that all joy lies in achieving through thinking becomes indifferent to applause—yes, and to censure.

Have I a mind? I have not, my mind has me!

Thinking about Thinking

Indeed, I am my mind; I am nothing else. Everything else I think I am is just that—merely what I think I am. Everything outside me is to me what I think it is. You know this; I am merely reminding you of it. If I have no thoughts about a thing, it does not exist for me. By deliberately cultivating constructive thoughts about an idea I bring that idea into concrete existence. Bringing things into existence is the chief end of man; and whether he thinks so or not, whether he believes it or not, he is forever creating in his thoughts. It is not merely man's business to create; it is his nature; it is his mission; it is his pastime. He can't help creating!

Do we create evils? Certainly; all the evils there are—just by thinking evil. Do we create good? Assuredly; simply by thinking good. All thought is constructive. "There is nothing either good or bad, but thinking makes it so." We construct destruction when we think destruction. We create war by thinking about it. We create what we do not like by thinking about what we do not like—sickness, trouble, poverty. If you do not believe these statements, you cannot think long about them—really think, honestly think—without becoming convinced. Do we create happiness and health and wealth by thinking about them? Of course—by straight thinking.

But what is straight thinking? Another name for intellectual honesty. What is intellectual honesty? It is looking squarely at any subject, seeing it as truly, as frankly, as unequivocally, as selfforgetfully as we can. It is seeing a thing without allowing any outside consideration to influence our vision of the truth about it. It is simply allowing our intelligence and imagination to take hold of truth as we know it.

We all know the truth when we see it. And we can see it by looking for it. The ability to see it is a divine gift—or a natural endowment, if you prefer the term. The truth for me about any given subject may be that I do not know the subject; but I know the truth. If I start there and think honestly about that subject, I shall soon see some of the truth about it. If I think about it long enough and steadily enough and single-heartedly enough, I shall learn much truth about it. I may find it expedient to turn to outside sources for short-cuts in my process—to learn what other men have thought about it. But if I am thinking truly, I accept only those thoughts of other thinkers that measure up to my standard of the truth. No authority for me unless his thoughts do measure up.

Genius is clear vision of truth—nothing more nor less. Masterpieces are the visible and tangible expressions of great visions of truth. Carlyle said, "Genius is an immense capacity for taking trouble"; there is also a popular saying that "genius is hard work." But genius is neither; it is only in the expression of genius in words or in works that infinite pains are requisite. Say infinite care, rather! The vision itself, if it is clear enough to rank as genius, will force one to infinite care in its perfect expression. But sheer genius forces the very form of the expression; and what appears to onlookers to be the hard work involved in expression is sheer joy to the expresser! Why? Because real thinking is sheer joy! Because right thinking is living in "the kingdom of God."

Men fail of expressing the vision of the truth only when they allow themselves to be influenced in their thinking by some consideration other than the expression of what they have seen. Fix your eyes on the effect that you aim to produce, and at once you are looking away from your vision of the truth and are ceasing to see it clearly. At best, you then see it obliquely, with consequent foreshortening, distortion, loss. Consider your phrases, and your attention is distracted. In this distraction lies the difference between the divine flashing of the truth and clever phrase making. And when and only when you attempt to be clever, the thing becomes work. Form dictated by an eye to opinion destroys itself. The moment any one bows to an authority outside himself, he blindfolds his inner eye and ceases to create. He becomes a mere assembler.

All art, all invention, all revelation, come through the inner eye; only outside considerations blind us to the true vision. Consideration of the critic's attitude toward the expression, of the editor's judgment, of the buyer's fancy, of the public's estimate, of the box-office results, of reputation, of reward, of fame, robs us of the ability to see!

Yet Truth is what the world strives for, pays for, weeps for. Because so few of us realize this, the world at times—at all times, perhaps—is starving for Truth. Because it cannot find the real thing, it grasps at the half-truth. But no man needs to starve for Truth; it is more plentiful and more accessible than bread. It comes plentifully to the man who discovers what fun it is to think; who realizes where the fun comes from when he is thinking. Every normal man is a potential genius, because it is divinely given him to see Truth, if he will, and to let it express itself through him in the form that it selects and shapes. The common man is a divine creature; he has only to let himself appear what he is, instead of trying to appear what he wants somebody else to think he is. We wreck the very genius of our children by forcing "considerations" upon them. We wreck our own supreme gifts by clinging to the considerations that somebody has imposed upon us.

We destroy the most marketable quality of what we have to sell by striving to put into it marketable qualities—by not realizing that we cannot paint the lily. We have only to pick it with infinite pains to preserve its perfection. Coal would burn no better if we gilded it. Wheat loses food value as it becomes white flour.

This idea is as old as the hills—and so is gold; but to each man who discovers it for himself it is forever new and marvelous, as is the fresh outcropping of precious metal to the old miner. Every human being carries around with him an unworked mine in which lie all the happiness, all the well-being, all the pleasure that he will ever get.

Here, then, is a formula: If you are not happy, try thinking. Let your mind select the subject that most fascinates it. Ask of your own mind the truth about that subject. The greatest question that the human mind ever formed is "Why?" Insist on having the truth. Dodging an issue is blinding the inner eye and spoiling the vision. Put every preconceived opinion about your subject to the acid test of this inner assay. Submit authority, your own and that of others, to the searchlight of your own utterly honest analysis. Remember that it is no part of your job to put in his place somebody who disagrees with you. Pitch sophistry on the scrapheap. Ask yourself the whys of the thing. Face every question that arises out of it; dig up every doubt about it and answer it squarely; turn up its pleasant and its unpleasant aspects, its flattering and its unflattering elements; look through it and around it. If you find inconsistencies with your first conclusions, recognize that one or other of your conclusions is necessarily wrong; for there are no inconsistencies between truths and all differences can be reconciled. Because Truth is one—indivisible whole, omnipresent, omnipotent. Truth is God.

What will happen to you? I think you will discover that you are having more fun than you can find in any other pursuit. You will find that you cannot let thinking alone. You will see that other men are constructed the same way—you will understand them better. But what is more, "you'll be a man, my son," as Kipling says; you will find yourself. You will find independence. You will find your own relation to men and things. You will find your own wisdom, which the Creator meant you to have. You will find your own taste; you will find your own bent; you will find health; you will find what you have to sell that the world wants. You will find your own religion. You will not find all the truth about the subject that you started with, because all the truth about anything leads invariably to infinity. But you will find your job—for eternity. You will find enough to transform your life. It matters not what you start thinking about, philanthropy, glass-blowing, locomotives, highway robbery, ship biscuit, life insurance, or fish bait. The Spirit of truth will lead you into more Truth; and finding Truth is fun—the only fun there is; and it is the highroad to anything else you want, if you want anything else.

Do you think this is a simple treatment of a tremendous theme—simple to the verge of rashness? Precisely so. Truth is a simple thing for simple minds. The skeptical world, at every fresh presentation of Truth, itself always puts its sneering slur in just those words, thereby proving exactly the main contention herein offered. Finding Truth by thinking is the natural, instinctive amusement of truly simple minds. Simplicity is the essence of the only terms on which Truth will be had. "Know what you mean, and you'll be great," Barrie says. And the simple mind, seeing the simple Truth and simply expressing it, thereby becomes great. And the whole of this or any other statement is only true for you or me in so far as it measures up to our standard. It is not what authority says is true, but Truth that is the only authority! "I would rather be right than be President!" Why? It is more fun; and incidentally, the road to the presidency of—anything!

Ideas in Trust

THERE IS A REMARKABLE little book called "Finding Youth," by Gertrude Nelson Andrews, that tells the story of a man who lost his position when he was sixty years of age, after a lifetime of faithful service to others. In despair, he did not know which way to turn to make a living for himself and his beloved wife. In his own trade, printing, no place was open for him; and he knew no other trade. Want and the shame of failure stared him in the face. But through the chain of circumstances that makes up the body of the story, he found in himself a creative faculty, which he began to use. He found that by giving attention to this creative urge he could reconstruct his work and his life. He found that by giving heed to its suggestions and dictates he could reconstruct his youth. And he did. He built a new career for himself, and happiness and prosperity.

The author tells me this story is not fact but fiction. It doesn't matter, for whichever it is, it is true. Man does have a creative faculty in him that will reconstruct his work and his career and his youth if he will pay attention to it and obey it. Every woman has creative ability that she could use, if she would, to remake her home, her family relations, her domestic happiness, her out-

Ideas in Trust

side career. The trouble is that we do not usually trust this inner urge to create. We haven't any confidence in our own ideas—because they are our own.

Maybe you think this is not true in your case. But stop and review some of your experiences. Don't you often look at some device or plan or fabrication that somebody else has made and see a better way of doing it? Don't you sometimes know there is a better way, and aren't you sure it could be worked out if more time were given to it? Don't you frequently believe you could build a house, run a school, launch a business, sail a boat, play bridge, raise radishes—anything whatever that happens to interest you—better than somebody else you see doing it, if you only had time to gain the requisite fundamental information with which to equip your creative impulses?

And haven't you had the experience of thinking of what seemed momentarily a good idea; then discarding it because it was your own and so couldn't be worth much—and soon after finding that somebody else had conceived the selfsame idea, used it, put it over successfully, and reaped the profits and the credit that might have been yours? And how cheap you felt, when all you could say to yourself was "I thought of that first. Why didn't I do it?"

I know a man who had the idea for the internal-combustion engine—gasoline engine—long before it was put on the market, but who never got round to working it out till somebody else "beat him to it." I knew the boy who invented the first fly swatter made of wire screen with a handle, and who made a few and sold them in the local hardware store in the town where he lived—and then let the device slip away from him because he did not value his own idea. And later—you know what happened—another man or men took the same idea and made a fortune out of it.

You know, it would be a good thing for every one of us about once a year, at least, to read over Russell Conwell's famous lecture "Acres of Diamonds" and Emerson's essay "Self-Reliance." Have you ever read them? Could you read them without a tremendous stir inside of you urging you to go and do the thing that you wanted to do, carry out your idea, build your structure, execute your plan, win your prize? Well, as Emerson says in that very essay, that is the creative urge within you stirring for expression. And that very urge, in the man or woman who pays attention to it, is the source of achievement and fortune and fame and usefulness—and the only source; because it is the voice of the Spirit offering guidance, just as much and just as truly as conscience, rebuking our mistakes, is the same voice dealing with another theme.

The English writer A. C. Clutton-Brock has written two books that every Truth student could well afford to read. One is called "What Is the Kingdom of Heaven?" and the other "Studies in Christianity." In one of them he calls attention to the fact that every person has within him what might be called an "artistic conscience" that tells him what is beautiful. And he goes on to say that this is the voice of the Spirit within. Then he argues that this same voice tells us also what is true in experience, as surely as the ear tells us the true ring of genuine silver coin. The same voice tells us what is right, what is kind, what is honest. And it is the same voice that tells us what to do, and how to do it; that urges us to create useful, beautiful, amusing, delightful things. And if we only would listen! Oh, it's *the* tragedy of life that we don't listen!

Perhaps it is your own personal tragedy at this moment that you are refusing, or neglecting, to listen to the voice that is telling you exactly what would get you out of your troubles and into your highest happiness, if you would only obey. And maybe you haven't "the courage of your own ideas," maybe you think they are no good because they are yours. Perhaps it never really occurs to you to trust them, because they are yours. Perhaps you tremblingly guess that they might be some good if only somebody else thought so, but you don't dare to propound them or execute them or work on them—because they are yours.

But oh, my friend, they are not yours! They are simply offered you for use—like everything else we call our own in this world. And they—these ideas that press upon us for utterance or expression—they are not merely something we have the privilege of expressing; we have an obligation to express them. We have the option—oh, yes!—the option whether we will express them or not. We have the option whether we will do something worth while in the world's thinking, in invention, in industry—or remain merely followers and trailers of the men and women who do use their ideas, and lead.

Now the purpose of all meditation, of all going into the silence, of all listening for the voice, is to receive ideas. Sometimes ideas pop into our mind when we are not consciously seeking them. Sometimes they come as the result of deliberate seeking for them. Sometimes they come promptly and easily; sometimes after long labor and "cudgeling of brain." And sometimes they come after we have given up the effort to get them—they just rise up out of the subconscious mind, like people whom we have invited to dinner and who come after we have given up expecting them.

Some of us study this operation of going into the silence, yearning and longing for the rewards that it promises yet utterly overlooking the ideas that come to us in our silent thought, just because they are not exactly what we expected.

I knew a man who was working on an invention. His purpose was so dear to him that he began to think that it might be wrong in him to cherish it. He was a student of Truth, and so tried to practice the silence to learn what was right for him to do. But he found that whenever he tried to get still and listen, all he would get would be a mind full of seething ideas for his invention. He tried desperately to crowd them out of his thoughts, to think only of abstract good, to look for abstract guidance; but he found himself helpless against the inrush of ideas for his invention. Finally, in despair, he turned away from his efforts after "guidance" and went back to working out his invention, using with half a sense of guilt some of the ideas that had come to him when he was trying to "meditate." And lo, his invention began to work out and ultimately became a success, and the inventor prospered. And then one day he woke up to the fact that all the time the voice had been trying to tell him exactly what he wanted most to know, while he himself had been trying desperately not to listen —or rather trying desperately to hear something else that he thought he ought to hear.

That is a great trouble with many of us. We try so hard to hear something we think we ought to hear, or something we simply want to hear, that we fail to hear the actual voice at all. Inspiration—your own creative urge—waits in your heart, and it will transform your life, your career, your happiness, your prosperity if you will only listen and let it. It will tell you what you want to know or how to learn what you want to know. Sometimes it will tell you to go and learn what other people have learned and said or written about your problem. Sometimes it will tell you to go to work and do the best you can, and trust for results. Sometimes it will give you a great flash of illumination, with the whole plan of your enterprise complete in a picture before your inner eye. But usually it works for you a step or two at a time—and works as you work. Goethe, the famous German poet, expressed in a familiar verse one of the best of all methods of getting ideas, namely illumination, guidance:

"Are you in earnest? Seize this very minute,
What you can do, or dream you can, begin it;
Boldness has genius, power, and magic in it.
Only engage, and then the mind grows heated;
Begin, and then the work will be completed."

That verse has a world of inspiring helpfulness in it. Goethe seemed to know how God likes to work with us. God has a way of helping us when we start to do something for ourselves. We get along better when we begin. We obey the commandments, the urge, the inspiration—begin to obey—and then the reward begins to come. Try that way. Results will surprise you.

Of course, we don't rush to work things out in wood, or steel, or marble, or printed page, until we have first worked them out in mind. But—begin! Begin with the execution of the first glimmer of your idea. And often it will seize the pencil, or the chisel, or whatever the implement or instrument of your craft may be, and do the thing for you—or seem to do it for you—and amaze you with the usefulness or beauty, or both, of the product. Trust the voice, believe in the idea, begin to work it out. There's magic in it!

WORKING WITH GOD

Self-Expression

WE HEAR OFTEN ENOUGH that education is the bringing out of the pupil's ideas —inducing him to express himself or, better, leading him to let the Spirit of truth within him express itself through him. I hear that my work in life is to express God; to let God express Himself through me. I believe that, and I try to act upon it because I accept the idea that this power, in which I live and move and have my being *is* God. Certainly this is the power I call God. So God's attitude toward me is that of trying to induce me to express Him. As I try to express His attributes, love, truth, life, wisdom, power, I invite God Himself to express Himself through me.

Perhaps this idea will be clearer if we state it in another way. It occurs to me that the greatest happiness, yes, the keenest pleasure—if pleasure is what I want—is this expression of my self. God gives me that pleasure by inducing me to express myself. I learn tremendously as I endeavor to express myself; I become astonishingly happy; I find myself irresistibly attracted to God, because He lets me express myself. And these things being perfectly obvious to me, it becomes suddenly obvious, too, that God's method is a singularly good one; that if He gives me education, delight, pleasure, by leading me to express myself, I shall be expressing Him still further and still better if I adopt His method with any one whom I want to help. Instead of laying down laws, preaching, arguing, why do I not try to induce my friend, my pupil, my wife, my child, to express himself? Why not try to help him bring out his own ideas and make them appear to him to be his own discovery, his very own? As a matter of fact, they will be, must be of his own thinking if they are ever to be his at all. I can only induce him to work the mine that is in his own heart and to find the treasure that already belongs to him.

How intensely practical is this method in everyday affairs! It is said that the way to become popular is to become a good listener. What is a good listener? A good listener is one who induces another to express himself, is he not? The road to popularity! Not a high goal, you say, popularity? Why not? To be truly popular is to be loved. If you love, you cannot avoid a return in kind. If you would have influence, you must in a sense be popular. So this method of God's is a road to popularity with my friend, with my wife, and with my child, with my pupil, with my boss, with my customer, with myself! A chance for self-expression is the chief delight of man's existence, and every one of us recognizes that fact in one way or another. We yearn to express ourselves, and we insist on expressing ourselves in various ways, from the low forms

Self-Expression

of garrulity, strutting, and posing, to the high forms of uttering great truths in science, in art, and in other ways. Perhaps the highest form of self-expression may be the inducing of another to express his true self. After all, maybe I accomplish that when I express the highest Truth that I find within myself.

Suppose I am a sculptor and make a wonderful statue that expresses the everlasting truth that is in beauty. I thereby induce every one who sees my work with appreciation to express, in his very appreciation, something of that same truth, do I not? I *am* a sculptor, carving a statue of character to express all that I can of the truth of God's infinite beauty. My very purpose in carving the statue must be to express God so that others will express Him in their appreciation. That sounds like a bold statement, but look at it in the light of Jesus' command "Let your light shine." Of course my purpose is to win appreciation not for my little "lower-case" self, but for the true beauty that I express.

The successful teacher is he or she who leads the pupil to express the self within. A teacher becomes great in proportion as he leads his pupil to the greatest self-expression. Education is the bringing out of the pupil's powers.

Sometimes we hear people say, "I'm going to teach that fellow a lesson," implying that the intention is to make the lesson a bitter one. If such an idea occurs to me, I should do well to stop and consider whether the lesson is really one that I wish to teach. If it is, the only way to teach it is to bring out in that person the power to grasp the idea that I want him to grasp. I cannot bring the idea home to his mind by any other process.

And when I wish to teach another a lesson it might be well for me to stop and make sure that I know the lesson myself. A lesson in justice cannot be taught by injustice; a lesson in mercy cannot be taught by cruelty; a lesson in humility cannot be taught by arrogance! A good lesson cannot be taught by a method that is not good; it cannot be taught if the teaching is accompanied with any emotion or feeling that is not good. Good can be conveyed only lovingly, and love teaches no one a lesson with intent to make it bitter.

By the same token, God, who is love, will teach me no lesson with intent to make it bitter. God tries to induce me to express Him and to look for His expression in everybody and in everything. Where I look for God, I find Him.

Expressing God—that is my whole work in life. What is expressing God? It is letting His attributes, life, love, wisdom, power, Truth, flow through me into the visible. I am eager that God should express Himself through me as health and prosperity. Then all I have to do is to let Him express Himself as love and Truth. For God is not a group of separate attributes: He is one, all His attributes a perfect whole, inseparable, and I cannot let one attribute flow through me to ex-

Self-Expression

pression without allowing the others to be manifested also. If I let love and Truth seep through me, health and prosperity will seep with them; if I let love and Truth gush through an unblocked channel, health and prosperity will gush with them. God Himself cannot send part of His attributes through me; He must send all or none. I cannot express Truth without expressing wisdom. If I would be well, I have but to serve and to be kind and true. If I express any attribute of God perfectly, the other attributes will be expressed proportionately.

So, if it is the way of God to induce me, to encourage me to express Him, how better can I express Him than by adopting His way and encouraging expression in everybody with whom I come in contact? And if I help others to express God, the instant result is that God expresses Himself again through them to me.

If I want God to speak through my mouth, I must first let Him think through my intelligence. If I will let Him, God will speak for me, think for me, decide for me, act for me, pray for me. The only real speaking, thinking, deciding, living, praying, is God's, because the only life, love, wisdom, power in me to do any of these things is God in me. Let Him? Why, all I have to do is to look inside instead of outside for everything.

It is men's feeling that supply is uncertain that makes them grasping. A sense of God's abundant provision of everything needed for each one of His creatures, and a realization that all His creatures' interests are common interests makes grasping not only unnecessary, but clearly absurd.

The path to all my good is through recognition of the omnipresence of God, the good.

If I fail to see good everywhere, in everything, all the time, I shall certainly not realize good in all my affairs. Good—God—only *is* for me where I recognize it—or Him.

We have talked about expression; it has often been said that we know God only by expressing Him. How true this is no one can realize till he begins trying to express God consciously. Of course, I express God unconsciously continually, because "in him we live, and move, and have our being." But consciously expressing Him in one way leads me to a consciousness of His expression through me in other ways. If I consciously express love, I become aware that love is wisdom, and that I am expressing wisdom when I express love. Presently I come to see that by expressing love and wisdom I find power. And suddenly I become conscious that the expression of love, wisdom, and power is the expression of life. I see that these so-called attributes of God are inseparable, even if I do not see that they are synonymous. As I go on in my conscious experience, I shall find constantly growing a consciousness that they are synonymous.

Now, as I express the attributes of God, I begin to be aware of the same attributes "expressing back" to me. I cannot be kind to a dog that he does not give me his friendship. I cannot care for a flower that it does not bloom more richly for me. I cannot deal truthfully with men that they do not begin to reciprocate by dealing honestly with me. I cannot turn a friendly face to the world that the world does not begin to be friendly to me. And suddenly again I realize that these attributes of God are elsewhere besides in me. As I deal with natural laws, I find that when I obey them they always work for my good. As I deal with mathematics, I find that if I abide by the principles, the result is always perfect. Presently I begin to see that good—God—is everywhere, in everything to which I turn in the right spirit.

What is the right spirit? Why, this spirit of giving out what I want to receive. Expressing! Expressing the divine attributes to the glory of God.

Every experience in life sooner or later is resolved into terms through which this principle becomes visible as its basis. So, when I reach this point, I find that if I want to realize the omnipresence of God—the realization that is my salvation and my heaven—I have only to make God omnipresent in everything I give out, everything I do, say, think. That will prove God's omnipresence to me immediately.

Stated in another way, it sounds startling. I have something to do with making God omnipresent! God cannot be omnipresent without me! I have everything to do with making God omnipresent for me.

"What?" you exclaim. "Do you control God?"

Why yes, in degree. I am God in expression —I am that spark of God which is expressing itself in me, which is individualized in me. I find God coming back to me in every return expression that my giving brings to me! Do you doubt that, O timid one, who cringes and whimpers before the idea of a God of terror who stands apart from you, outside of you, awaiting an opportunity to smite you for daring to take Him at His word? Then let us go back and read the Bible in which the truth is unmistakably told us; and realize again that it is truths like this about you and me that make the Bible true, and that it is not the fact that they are in the Bible that makes them true!

Startling thoughts, indeed! But they have brought us to the great fundamental truth of being. I am one with God, I am a spark of the divine, the same as God—His son, His heir. I am not separate from God. All that God is, I am; all that God has, I have! In limited degree? you insist. Yes; but I see no limit. I shall never see a limit.

But see what a marvelous law this is, this simple little law of giving and receiving! I am perfectly sure that all I have to do is to begin living by it, and it will lift me to the heights, bodily, mentally, spiritually! It will give me wings! It will transfigure and translate me! See how marvelously wise was that simple man of Nazareth when He said so simply that what we

Self-Expression

want to have done to us we have only to do to others! That was no moral epigram; it was a statement of law! How our realization of the wondrous beauties of the law of life, of the universe, expands as we come into this understanding.

This is heaven. Heaven is where God is. Who is God? God is intelligence, Truth, life, love. Wherever we find God—good—is heaven. When I find God everywhere, heaven is everywhere for me. But one of the little understood phases of Truth is that if I persist in finding God—good—in things nearest me, I shall begin to see Him in widening circles. It's like starting a fire in the grass, here at my feet. It will spread and grow with ever-increasing speed and power—and light!

Sometimes people who do not see this vision call people who do see it fanatics. I have done so. But a fanatic is one who grows enthusiastic over something he sees—that is, as he is observed from the standpoint of one who does not see. Looking through a telescope I become enraptured with the beauty of the stars. Or looking through the microscope I become enthralled by the wonders of cells. To one who does not look through or understand my instrument, I am a fanatic. Observing merely my reactions, he easily calls me an insane fool, which is what he means when he calls me a fanatic. And looking through the lens of spiritual vision, and seeing God omnipresent—oh, yes, in the stars and in the cells alike! in myself and in you!—I grow fanatical in the eyes of my neighbor who is ignorant of the lens, or ignores it! God help him! But is there anything surprising or unnatural about it? You don't blame a miner for shouting in mad delight when he discovers gold. Well, why shouldn't I be fanatically joyous when I look into heaven?

What is heaven? The sum total of perfection —whatever you like! Wouldn't you be a fanatic?

Would you like to find it, too? Well, begin looking for the omnipresence of God; looking first to see His presence in all that you say, do, or think—in what you give out. Just do unto others as you want them to do to you. It is just as simple as that!

Of course God *is* omnipresent; I merely become aware of it!

Waiting

IT IS ALMOST funny sometimes how we get ourselves all primed with good purposes—to love and trust, to give out what we want to get back, to do unto others what we want them to do unto us—and then the minute we find some "trouble" bobbing up in an unexpected way we get all upset, and confused, and scared, and grasp at the first expedient that suggests itself for combating infringement upon our rights, for getting our own way, for avoiding humiliation, for "saving our face." It would be funny if it weren't so tragic! How we do despair at our failures! when we ought to laugh—at ourselves.

It seems sometimes that when troubles face us, our first impulse is to fight, resist, snarl, scratch, bite, strike, crush. We find it hard to understand why. We grow desperate with a sense of our own unregenerate condition—our ingrained wickedness—our wretched inconsistencies.

If you are like me, or rather if I am like you—which I am inclined to believe I am—we both often wish that we could find some idea that we could cling to, some phrase that we could repeat, some reminder of our principle that we could use on all occasions when "trouble" appears, and that would start us off just right in dealing with it—some formula or recipe for immediate "first aid" that we might act upon until we had time to think, until we could bring up our reserves of experience and conviction and seasoned wisdom. Sometimes I think that that is what everybody wants most— a formula—a brief rule—for first aid.

I've found one that helps me. Maybe it will help you. It is "No hurry—wait!"

That "haste makes waste" is an old aphorism. A common observation upon the person who says or does unkind, mean, or cruel things on the spur of the moment—without "malice aforethought" is that he is "hasty." Hasty words, hasty acts, make trouble. Why? Because they are usually said or done without reference to the Spirit within —in disregard of the still small voice.

Of course there are impulsive speeches and deeds that are good. There are instantaneous responses to unexpected situations that are exactly right. There are sound decisions that lose nothing by being swift. But these are quite different from things done in a hurry. And rare indeed is the case in which it would not have been better to wait—until we knew what was right. Some wise man has said that nothing is ever lost by patience. We know that much is often lost by rush. To rush is rash.

As a matter of fact, it is hurry that causes most accidents. It is hurry that causes most disagreements. It causes most misunderstandings. It causes most disappointments. Hurry distracts the mind from clear thought. It drowns out the Voice. Hurry rimes with worry—and belongs in the same category. We say of a man who hurries and worries, that he gets "all hot and bothered" —and he does. And that is usually about all he gets. Unless he gets into a mess.

But think. People who do really great things never hurry. Nobody who writes a great book ever hurries. The great surgeon never hurries. The pilot of a great ship never hurries. The effective public speaker never hurries. Hurry never made a friend. It defeats the lover. Hurry never builds safely.

Hurry blinds the eyes to beauty. It destroys accuracy in the hand. It ruins judgment. It slurs action. Hurry is what causes heart failures and nervous prostrations. It overlooks the important things and sees only the trifles.

Hurry does nothing but defeat or delay you— in all sorts of things, all the way from shaving or dressing to closing the big deal or accomplishing the great result or giving the great performance or creating the great work.

No hurry—wait.

What shall we wait for? Well, in the 42d Psalm, as the Moffatt translation has it, we find, "Wait, wait for God." And not satisfied with saying it once, the Psalmist repeats it, "Wait, wait for God." And then in the 43d Psalm he says it again, "Wait, wait for God." Well, why should I not wait for God? He is the only power that will ever give me what I want, and what He gives is worth waiting for, isn't it?

Why hurry? Why hurry even when some

other driver tries to steal the right of way from me? Why hurry when somebody says something disagreeable to me? Why hurry when an obstacle looms in my path? Why hurry to do something the Voice has not suggested or approved? Hurry picks green apples, trips over the rug, breaks the point of the pencil. Hurry runs the boat aground, breaks the dish, burns the finger, leaves something out of the recipe, spills the ink, wastes the gas, drives past the address, barks the shin, rakes the fender, burns out the fuse, offends others, hurts their feelings, rushes in where angels fear to tread.

God never hurries. Nobody knows how long the universe has been in building. He seems to take eternity as the basis for His deliberation. Being His child in the midst of my own eternal life, why should I not be deliberate? Not that God does not move swiftly. He turns the earth at the rate of a thousand miles an hour. He sends it through space at many times that speed. He sends His sunlight traveling 186,000 miles a second. What do I know about speed? Well, there is one department in my life where I know speed—without hurry.

I think swiftly. I cannot help thinking swiftly. My thought is the swiftest thing I know anything about. It is swifter than light. It can travel to the outermost frontier of the universe and back, millions of millions of miles, in less time than it takes light to travel a mere 186,000 miles. Why am I in such a hurry to act, when I can think so quickly? Can't I afford to wait for thought?

But what *is* thought? Thought is the creative power in me, which is God Himself within me. Pure thought that is—unclouded, unobscured by fear. Hurry is always the expression of fear— fear that I shall be late, fear that I shall miss something, fear that I shall be defeated, or humiliated. It befogs thought. That is why it is thoroughly destructive. Hurry will not wait for thought—the creative power of God in me. Hurry will not wait for God. It is afraid God will be too slow in taking care of my interests, in defending me, in saving me from danger or from shame. Hurry is a mad impulse to beat the speed of light, the speed of thought, with physical action. Hurrying might be compared, then, to trying to pull "the limited" with a tortoise! Like trying to deliver the radio message in a wheelbarrow!

Hurry is the slowest way of doing anything. It is the worst way in the world to deal with emergency—which is another name for what we commonly call trouble. To hurry is to blindfold the eyes to vision and stop the ears to the Voice. To wait is to listen, to think. But you can think— millions of millions of miles, across the world and back, and around and back, and across the universe and back, and straight through to God—all in the time it takes you to step on the accelerator, or utter the curse, or strike the blow. Which is better? Why not step on the brake, shut the lips, withhold the hand?

But somebody has said, "He who hesitates is

lost." And somebody else avers that "opportunity knocks but once." Lies, both of them. He who hesitates, in the sense of waiting for God, is wise. Opportunity knocks continually, forever. He who hesitates to wait for God is lost. Opportunity to hear the Voice is opportunity. Hurry is delay—always serious, sometimes terrible. To wait is to appeal to speed—to the speediest thing we know—creative thought—God.

Just think how God waits—for you and for me.

Holy or Human?

"You try so hard to be holy that you forget to be human."

That criticism was leveled at one of the most sincere church workers I know, the other day. I winced for him, because perhaps the same thing might be said to so many of us by some of our critics, if they were frank with us.

I got to thinking about it in the night. Do I have to be holy or human? Is it inhuman to be holy, or is it superhuman? I believe it is neither. Humbly, I believe the effort to be holy is the highest and best I can make, and certainly I am not very successful at it if I make the very people I want to help think that I am less than human.

Holy means "whole." That's the original Anglo-Saxon of it. It is from the old word *hal*, long *a*, which according to our way of saying it now would be "hale." To be holy is to be hale, and surely there can be nothing less, or more, than human about that.

I think sometimes that some of us build barriers between ourselves and others around us by being too sober and somber and grave and solemn about our chief concern, which is living a life. I know a splendid man, a minister of the gospel, who preaches some of the best sermons I have listened to for years, but who solemnly shakes his head over us almost the whole time that he is presenting his message. It is as though he either thought that we are a hopelessly bad lot; or is fearfully impressed with the awful prospect of life and death and eternity; or thinks it's going to be "a narrow squeak" for the human race to climb out of its present Slough of Despond. It makes no difference whether his sermon is a warning of wrath to come or a joyous promise of peace on earth and good will to men: he solemnly shakes his head.

Sometimes it is laughable, sometimes it is almost unendurable even to those who are predisposed to like everything this fine man says. I know it drives good people out of the pews. I confess that it has been a strong influence to keep me out of church on some Sabbath mornings.

And, I wonder, do I get solemn like that over my references to religion, to my relations with my Creator, to my prospects of future life, or to present work? If so, why? To be holy means to be whole, and to be whole means to be sound. I do not believe it is sound to be solemn over anything in our faith. I believe in a God who cares about me, who guides me, who provides for me, for my present and for my future. Why should I be solemn about that? I believe in a God who overcomes evil with good and who will ultimately overcome all evil with good. Why should I be solemn over that? I do not like depressions, and I do not like rackets, and I do not like liquor, and I do not like ruthless financing. There are ever so many things that I do not like, but I am told that "all things work together for good to them that love God." I see no reason for getting gloomy about that.

I notice that when the saintly man or woman —or, let us say, the pious one—is presented on the stage or the screen, usually there is a strong tendency to caricature his or her solemnity. Why is it? You know the clever caricaturist or cartoonist picks out the most prominent feature in the face he cartoons, and emphasizes that till he makes his victim comic or ridiculous. It must be that solemnity is our "religious look." If that kind of heavy gravity in a man whom I respect and honor makes me react unfavorably towards him, what sort of reaction do I induce in the average man, to whom I am just one more Christian?

Of course the stage and the movies are frequently unfair to us, but no comment they make upon us could stick if the feature they cartoon were not prominent in us.

If I have any confidence in the faith that I profess, would not a cheerful attitude in the face of troubles be the most convincing thing I could offer to the men and women whom I want to influence? To be sure, a professionally cheerful attitude is about as offensive as gloom, maybe more so. But why shouldn't I be genuinely cheerful? Do I not believe that the promises are to be depended upon? "Trust in the Lord, and do good;

so shalt thou dwell in the land, and verily thou shalt be fed." "Delight thyself also in the Lord; and he shall give thee the desires of thine heart." It surely is not human to believe in such things as these, and then be gloomy about our belief. Maybe that's what our critics think.

Shall We Be Different?

THE POOREST REASON in the world for doing anything is that somebody else is doing it. Children have a name for the imitator; they call him a "copy cat." But isn't it a curious thing that the "copy cat" habit is almost universal among human beings? What? Do I think I am not a slave to it? Don't I wear that monstrosity known as the derby hat, when it is "in," and don't I laugh at it when it is "out"? Don't I fence my lawn when my neighbor does—and take the fence away when he razes his? Don't I say the same things about newspapers, relatives, and sunsets that the leaders in my particular club, set, or party say? Don't I rise, sit, sleep, and eat as others do? Isn't it one of my aims in life not to be queer—that is, unlike others?

Isn't it pitiful! I conform. I conform to style, to custom, to mode, to trend!

As I think about it I come upon a curious anomaly. The world cries out for originality—for something new under the sun—yet slaps at it instantly when it raises its head. No one is so unpopular as he who begins to be unlike the rest. But no one receives such rewards as he who persists in it! Strange! All men seem to be in a conspiracy to curb originality, yet all men laud and reward it. And then when the applause begins, they all begin trying to ape the originator.

An old song, attributed to New York dwellers, carried these lines:

> "Of course you may never be like us,
> But be as like us as you possibly can!"

People laughed at it, but they obeyed its behest. In America there is a strange worship for what is done and said and approved and successful in New York. Nothing else will make success for a drama, or a fashion, or a slang phrase, or a salad, or a trick doll, or a pipe, or a fad of any sort, like a widespread report that it is a success or a fad in New York. And New York imitates Paris, and Paris imitates Vienna—or did—and styles run in cycles when there is nothing left for style to imitate but itself; and we idolize antiques, and history repeats itself, all for the same reason. And then, along comes a man or a woman who thinks, sees an inward vision, departs from custom, manner, and convention, and is first persecuted, then hailed as a new leader for a new epoch—and becomes something to imitate again.

It has been said that genius is "smashing the rules." That may be an inadequate definition; most definitions are inadequate. But it is a fact that no genius ever observes the rules. The rules? What are they? Summed up, they would read: "Do as I do, and depart not, lest you become conspicuous."

And herein is another marvel. Most of us seek fame, reputation, the limelight, notoriety;

Shall We Be Different?

yet we fear to become conspicuous because of a difference in our neckties or in the cut of our evening clothes. Constantly we strive to lead, yet forever we trail. We dream of the world's eyes turning our way, yet we strive to remove every reason why they should. We are as like as the successive impressions of the proverbial rubber stamp, which differ only as they grow paler after the inking!

What does it all mean? It means not only that we are following a method that is wholly wrong, but it means also that we are flinging away our birthright, the one thing that makes us worth while, the one thing that makes us men, the one thing that proves us to be sons of God! We are flinging away the inner leading and looking outside for everything, from the shapes of our forks to our moral standards.

Least of all do we dare to be different in our religion!

But let us not fall into an obvious error. Being different for the sake of being different is the height of folly—though one almost wishes to follow such a course when he grows suddenly soul-weary of conformity. The fact that most men drive on roads is no reason why I should drive in the fields. That most men live in houses should hardly suggest to me the advisability of living in a cave. Men have tried such methods in their search for originality. You see them doing it every day. People neither hate nor applaud that sort of being different; it is merely ridiculous.

But these are the very ones who bring discredit upon the whole idea of being different. Their idiosyncrasies and excesses cause us to shy away from all their ways.

However, the conclusion is obvious and inescapable. What other people do should set no standards for me. Therein lies one of the hardest of all lessons to learn. "For ye . . . like sheep" was no chance expression. Salvation itself lies in being different.

But how am I to take thought and be different, without being different for the mere sake of difference? I am between Scylla and Charybdis; how can I escape? There is but one way. I shall escape by turning from a wholly false standard to the true one. I shall find the true standard just where I find everything else that is true—in my own mind, if I will only look there, look steadily, and be willing to see.

It is said of Emerson that no matter what subject he started to speak or write upon, it always led presently to the presentation of his one great theme. The same is true of all of us. No matter where we start or which way we work with any given question, if we are honest it will always lead us to our great theme—consciousness of the omnipresence of God.

Do we need argument to convince us that God is everywhere and in everything? No; all we need is to look and see. He is here in this question of conformity compared to originality. And when I begin to see Him in the question, the question is

Shall We Be Different?

settled! No question can exist when I see it clearly; it becomes its own answer. When we all shall have clear vision of God, interrogation points will disappear from our type cases and from our language. So will periods. We shall have no doubts —and no finalities. If we still shall need printed signs, the only one that will have significance will be ∞, the sign of infinity!

It is characteristic of many wild animals that they rarely raise their gaze above the level of their own eyes. To be safe from attack by one of them a man has only to climb a tree, and watch the beast that stalks him pass blindly underneath. Isn't it a curious thing that man, observing and knowing such a thing, doesn't see the object lesson in it? Let us raise our eyes! I raise my gaze above the level of my eyes, and what do I see? Everything worth while. Am I a creature of a two-dimensional world that I should see nothing that has height? No; nor do three dimensions bound my vision. I see within. And there is where I find every true standard of life awaiting my discovery. What has "what others are doing" to do with me?

Real or Counterfeit

IT DOESN'T matter what anybody else thinks about all this. The relation between God and me is purely individual. I need no intermediary, and if I don't, surely God does not. Shall I follow any teacher? Yes, one; Jesus Christ. No other. Get light from every one and any one who has light for you. God sends His messages through many channels. But do not call yourself a disciple of any human being—nor be one. Do not depend on other human beings. Depend on the Christ within yourself.

Yes, it is quite true that what other people think often affects me greatly, if I do not have a care. People laugh at me for believing as I do. They sneer. They think I am a pretender, a fraud, because they cannot see what I see. Because they cannot see what I see, they conclude that it isn't there.

Other people have religious, philosophic, scientific faiths of their own, and they think I must be wrong because I do not think as they do. How should that affect me? Not at all—except to warn me not to get to thinking I am the only one who is right.

I see people prospering while to me they appear to be doing anything but right. Others who seem to be saints have neither health nor wealth nor happiness. What about them? I wonder if Jesus did not have them in mind—all of them, the wrong-headed and the right-intentioned—when He said, "Judge not."

How can I judge? I do not know another's circumstances, I do not know his habits, physical, mental, or spiritual. I do not know whether the apparent sinner is all wrong, or the apparent saint all right. I know I am neither, and that perhaps they are both somewhat like me.

I see people who work hard and accomplish nothing worth while. I see people who seem to loaf and yet achieve. But how do I know that the hard worker doesn't defeat himself by his thinking, and that the loafer's real work is done in his thought. I cannot judge either of them with any accuracy of course, so how can I judge the advice they may give me?

But the most dangerous critic I have among other people is the one who challenges me with "Physician, heal thyself." When I am not successful in solving all my own problems, when there are still obvious defects in my way of living, when I go directly contrary in practice to what I preach, then this critic finds me vulnerable indeed.

But should I mind? Is he injuring me? Isn't he really helping me—helping me to see how I might be a much better person than I am, how I might have a much finer experience than I am having, how I might rise to greater heights? His criticism may sound destructive, but if I see it as constructive, I shall simply gain by it—perhaps, immeasurably.

What makes me wince when I am criticized unfavorably? Well, probably the same thing that makes me glow when I am praised. Vanity. I can't stand criticism because I can't bear to have anybody think I am not a wonderful fellow. Well, what does that indicate? That I want people to think I am a wonderful person whether I am or not? What kind of an attitude of mind is that? It is not even common honesty that wants to be thought better than it is. If I try to make impressions on other people that do not represent the individual I really am, then I am a counterfeiter, am I not?

I am quick to see counterfeits in other people. I wonder if there is anything in the idea that we see in others only what is in ourselves.

Some writers have said that vanity is the chief of all human motives. Some moralists depend almost entirely upon their ability to appeal to the vanity of other people in efforts to influence them. Flattery is the main stock in trade of many a salesman. When we "fall for it," what does it make us out to be? Counterfeiters?

How quickly we should be warned of the weakness in ourselves, of the danger we are in, when either blame or praise affects us too much; particularly when we know that we do not deserve the praise or the blame, and when we begin to fear that we shall not get credit for something we have said or done that we think was well said or done. We shall sometimes be applauded, sometimes hissed, whatever we do. People will attempt to judge us. Sometimes they will be nearly right, sometimes wholly wrong. Should we be much affected by their verdicts? Probably the estimate others make of us is never accurate. Then if we accept it, knowing that it is not accurate, what do we become? Counterfeiters?

Sooner or later a counterfeit is always discovered for what it is. When the glitter is not really gold, when the metal is pinchbeck, when the fabric is shoddy, when the life belt is stuffed with sawdust, the gas mask made of *Ersatz*—eventually it appears. People know. "Be sure your sin will find you out" is no joke.

On the other hand, be sure your virtue will find you out, too. Not only should you not, but actually you can not, hide your light under a bushel.

There is a kind of modesty that is false, also there is a dishonest modesty, a modesty that evades facts, that tries to make itself out something it is not. Modesty as a mask is contemptible; modesty as a pretense is ridiculous. After all, why should I be modest? Why should I think about modesty at all? I shall not, unless I am consciously trying not to show my vanity!

No, no, we cannot mind what others think about us, or about anything else. That does not mean, of course, that we should be inconsiderate of their beliefs. Far from it. It does not mean that we should be intolerant of their opinions.

We haven't time to be either. Our business is to be loving, serving, trusting, going about doing good. What have vanity, or modesty, or fear of criticism to do with those aims? Not one thing. They belong to a world of false appearances, a world of counterfeits.

It all comes back to the same thing always. I am only concerned to be, to go, to do, to give—and not at all with anything else. I am not concerned with conditions, circumstances, environment. They will become all that heart can desire when I myself am right, and that means when I myself am genuine. How can I be genuine when I am full of pretense and the desire for approval? Why, "I can do all things through Christ which strengtheneth me." "The Father abiding in me doeth his works."

What will people think? "Public opinion!" Under a banner with that device we should be no better than slaves. What do *I* think? should be my standard. That is, what do I think deep down in the silence, at the bottom of my own heart, where my honest opinion of myself and all my works expresses itself in no uncertain terms. No shame will ever come to me from ridicule that will equal the sense of shame I suffer when my own heart tells me I am a fraud, a counterfeit. And no applause will ever be so sweet as the sense of rightness—spiritual health—that I get when my own heart tells me I am sound.

Kipling says that triumph and disaster are two impostors to be treated "just the same." That is never truer than when the triumph or disaster is to vanity. Vanity is the impostor of impostors. The archimpostor! It is the archswindler, the archcounterfeiter.

WORKING WITH GOD

Maps and Instructions

DID YOU EVER start out on a cross-country trip of a hundred miles or more, from a height which gave you a view of the whole road you had to travel, from beginning to end? It would be a high mountain indeed that would give you such a view. There are doubtless places in our Rockies from which we can see the country for long distances, sometimes perhaps for fifty miles, maybe much more. Sometimes the air is so clear that distant things seem much closer than they actually are. Sometimes we can actually see the road itself, its turns and twists, its straight stretches, its climbs and descents, its bridges, the towns along the way, even the detours, so far ahead that we can anticipate nearly all the conditions we shall have to meet on the way to where we plan to go.

But usually the road ahead of us is no such open path. Usually we get out the road map and study it, and lay out our route by what somebody else—the mapmaker—tells us is the most practical, the most direct, the easiest way. Then we get reports from some automobile club as to the condition of pavements, shortcuts, points of interest, places to find food and shelter, the safe, comfortable highways to follow—all based on actual experience in driving over the route we intend to follow. Then we watch the signs along the way: "Twelve Miles to Pleasantville," "Turn Right for Delight Valley," "This Way to Big Vision Mountain," "Slow—Sharp Turn," "Steep Hill—Go into Second Gear," "Crossroad," "School —Slow," "Men at Work," "Fresh Oil," "Toll Bridge Ahead," "Gingergas and Smoothoil," "Welcome to Ourtown," "Drive Carefully, Please," "Thank You." Road signs, these, put up by people who came this way before we did, and who made it their business or thought it a privilege to make the road safe and easy and pleasant for us!

All this for our guidance. All we have to do is to observe simply and follow instructions quietly and easily and naturally, and we "get along fine"! If we follow this guidance simply and naturally. Guidance!

But what do we do about guidance on a long, long road, very little of which we can commonly see from any height, the road we call life? Do we get a road map, ask people who know from experience, watch and obey the signs along the way?

Some of us do strange things. Some of us spend hours, weeks, years turning over road maps, skeptical concerning their dependability. Some of us distrust everybody who tells us his experience. Some of us "don't believe in signs." Some of us pull up beside the road and stop and wait and guess and worry. We seem to have an idea that some good angel is going to come along and take us in tow, or do our driving for us. Some of us just throw away all available information, release our brakes, step on the gas, and go roaring along reckless of curves and hills and traffic and crossroads and men at work and all the rest, as if luck were the rule of the road, as if we had a heaven-given right to think that some special dispensation of Providence might guard us from danger and carry us through. Then when things happen that we do not like, when "accidents" occur, or when nothing happens at all, or insurmountable obstacles oppose us, we grow sour, or bitter, or furious, or despairing, or resigned, and resent the fact that we have to travel the road at all, and abuse fate, or fortune, or God—whatever we think we believe in—for allowing us to suffer, for requiring anything of us, for putting us here in the first place!

Some of us do still stranger things. I know a man who spends his time telling other people how to travel the road, but who neglects his family, dodges obvious duties, borrows money without any idea of paying it back, changes his plan every few weeks, yet sets himself up as an authority on life and living. I know a woman who always picks out the hardest thing she can find to do and tries to do that, who is a martyr at every opportunity, who looks upon life as a vale of tears, who seems to think that getting to heaven is mostly a matter of dodging hell, and who considers it her duty, or right, or privilege to meddle in other people's affairs as if she had been divinely appointed to set them right by mixing them up. I know another man who professes to be searching for Truth, but who always puts up an argument against every idea that is presented to him. I know a man who has an ambition to achieve great things along a certain line of work, but who is always waiting for more favorable circumstances, for better ideas, for inspiration—and who devotes most of his time and effort to other things. I know boys and girls who profess to believe that everything in the way of maps and directions and signs is all "bunk." They go along "making whoopee," indulging in wild parties and getting over their effects, and sneering or making wise-cracks about everything that has even a flavor of seriousness about it. Yet they cynically assert that life is a mess, a chaos, a joke, a mystery, a meaningless experience, a mechanical torture device, a game of chance, a grab bag!

But let's use a little common sense. Isn't life a road that we should look upon exactly as we would look upon any other road we have to travel? In the first place, all of us want to go places and do things, don't we? All right, that means activity on our own part. If we don't want other people to get all our rewards, and have all our fun for us, we have to bestir ourselves. If we sit down idly, twiddle our thumbs, and wait, some fruit may fall into our lap, but not much. It requires activity, effort on my part just to enjoy eating, to dance, to play baseball or hockey or ping-pong or contract. I have to do something about it just to be well dressed or clean. I have to climb into bed just to sleep! Agreed?

Well, I want to go to the City of Happiness. The Great Mapmaker says that the only road is service. His instructions are "Love the Lord thy God with all thy heart, and with all thy soul, and with all thy strength, and with all thy mind; and thy neighbor as thyself." The only rule of the road that He stresses is "Whatsoever ye would that men should do unto you, even so do ye also unto them." He says, "Ask, and it shall be given you; seek, and ye shall find; knock, and it shall be opened unto you." And He adds, "Give, and it shall be given unto you."

Then, in case any of us might be in doubt at any time about just how to follow any of these simple instructions, He has given us a traveling companion that is called "the Spirit of truth," who "shall guide you into all the truth." He is the interpreter of my map and my instructions.

Very well. The name God means "good." I am to love the good with all there is in me. I am to treat my neighbor as I want him to treat me, not only giving him a square deal, but being as helpful to him as I can be, always. I am to act kindly toward him, speak kindly of him, think kindly about him—exactly as I want him to do toward me. Then I am to ask, seek, and knock actively in search of the things that are my heart's desires.

"Delight thyself also in Jehovah;
And he will give thee the desires of thy heart."

I am to give out what I want to get back. And

Maps and Instructions

when in doubt, I am to consult the Spirit of truth, who travels along with me in my heart.

Plain instructions, surely. The only thing that ever confuses me is how to consult the Spirit of truth. "Going into the silence" is a mystery to many of us. But it need not be if we just realize that it means not merely relaxing the body and calming the mind, though both are preparations for hearing the still small voice of Spirit. It means simply getting *honest* with ourselves. It means shutting out of the closet of a person's heart all the voices of self-deception, expediency, trickery, pretense, splurge, and letting the voice of Spirit tell him what really is good, what really is right, what really is kind, what really is giving. It means disregarding outside considerations of reward or punishment, and just trying genuinely to see what is Truth, with the purpose of doing the thing that is right and trusting God for the results. It means submitting a definite problem to Spirit, for His solution—not offering argument. It is quite true that sometimes Spirit, wise traveling companion that He is, will just smile at me, and say, "Look at your map" or "Review your instructions" or "Wait for road signs." Each and all are given me for guidance. But He will tell me the truth always—if that is what I want —about the road to happiness.

WORKING WITH GOD

Successful Trusting

THERE IS A KIND OF GIVING that sometimes seems harder to practice than any other, but that should be easier; namely, the giving of ourselves. Surrender.

It ought to be easy for me to give to God. To give Him my troubles, for instance, to give Him the responsibility for the result of my efforts. To give Him the care of my interests. To put my fortunes into His hands. To intrust Him with my health. And with my hopes.

It ought to be as easy as it is to give to Him all responsibility for developing the seed that I put into the ground. It should be as easy as trusting Him to keep the boat that I launch afloat. It should be as easy as trusting Him to see that I get nourishment from the food I eat.

But I find it hard to leave to God the responsibility of paying me for the work I do. I am afraid, perhaps, that somebody else besides God is going to have a good deal to say about the pay I get for what I do. Some human being who is unfair or grasping or jealous or ruthless may step in and declare that my work is not good enough, or is not of the right kind, or is not delivered in time, or should not be paid for at all. I am afraid that this person or that person may have more to say about whether I get paid, and how

Successful Trusting

much, than God will have to say. So I worry and fear and despair.

But what is the very essence of a belief in a loving Father? Isn't it faith that my Father cares about what happens to me? Isn't it faith that He wants things to be well with me, that He wants me to be well, that He wants me to be happy, that He wants me to be successful, that He wants me to be well paid for what I do? If that isn't what it means, then what does it mean?

God asks us to do two things, doesn't He? And only two things. Love and trust. Love Him and His other creatures; and trust Him for the result of loving. What else does He ask or command me to do? Aren't all the rest of our instructions simply echoes of these? Well, if that's all I have to do, what's hard about it? Don't I merely make it hard by thinking it must all be much more complicated than that? Don't I make it hard by trying to hang on to something more than that to do? Don't I cling to the idea that my whole duty cannot be comprised in any such easy, happy, delightful obligations as just loving and trusting? Isn't it my trouble that I can't quite bring myself to believe that results will come from just loving and trusting—results in terms of my heart's desires?

Well, if that is true, then I am not really surrendering to God, am I? I am still hesitant, trembling, afraid; and fear is certainly not trust.

Two articles appearing in *Unity* have expressed the idea of what trust is in a very wonderful way. One is "Let Go," by Elizabeth Hill, published in *Unity* in January, 1930; and the other "Lovingly in the Hands of the Father," by Evelyn Whitell, published in *Unity*, October, 1928, and subsequently in book form. The titles of these two expressions of the trusting spirit are in themselves revealing. "Let go" means just what it says. Don't try to hang on. "Lovingly in the hands of the Father" means putting it in His hands and leaving it there. As a matter of fact, when we have let go and left it lovingly in the hands of the Father, we have gone the whole way in trusting. There is nothing more we can do on that side.

The Bible is packed full of promises of what will happen to us when we trust. In the Moffatt translation—which puts the Bible in modern terms—in the 3d chapter of Proverbs, beginning with the 5th verse, we find,

"Rely with all your heart on the Eternal,
    And do not lean upon your own insight;
Have mind of him wherever you may go,
    And he will clear the road for you.

"Never pride yourself on your own wisdom,
    Revere the Eternal and draw back from sin:
That will mean health for your body and
    Fresh life to your frame.

"Honour the Eternal with your wealth, and
    With the best of all you make;
So shall your barns be full of corn, and your vats
    brim over with new wine."

Successful Trusting

What is there that is hard about that? Is it hard to rely with all your heart? Is it hard to "have mind of Him"? Is it hard to "revere the Eternal" or to "draw back from sin"? Is it hard to honor Him with your wealth? And if you will do those things, you are told that He will clear the road for you; He will give you health; He will give you abundant supply.

In the same version of the Bible, in the 62d Psalm, we find,

> "Leave it all quietly to God, my soul,
> My rescue comes from him alone;
> Rock, rescue, refuge, he is all to me,
> Never shall I be overthrown."

But do we leave it all quietly to God? Do we leave it *all* quietly to God? Our hopes and our fears, our aspirations and ambitions, our dreads and anxieties, our cares and our obligations, our successes and our failures, our tasks and our decisions, our abilities and our inspirations? Do we? How often do you catch yourself worrying about how to talk with some person about some interest of yours that you want to interest him or her in also? How often do you fear that you will say the wrong thing or won't think of the right thing to say? How often do you worry about the effect of what you have said or done, or left unsaid or undone? Have I made a sale? Have I won a friend? Have I persuaded an opponent? Have I made an enemy? Does that person like me? Will this person slander me? Shall I get credit for this piece of good work? Shall I be unfairly blamed for that? Shall I have enough money to pay my expenses next month, or next week, or tomorrow, or tonight? Can I afford to help this beggar? Can I take that vacation trip? Have I made a fool of myself? How can I meet this stranger? What do people think of me? How can I face this disappointment? What if so-and-so happens? Am I going to take cold? How can I stand that noise? Oh, if I were only anywhere else than here! Why haven't I the opportunity that this man has—or this woman? Why wasn't I born with outstanding ability? Is there really a God? Does He really care for insignificant, unworthy, worthless me? Are these the questions that are constantly seething in our mind?

When we turn over and over such thoughts as these, or thoughts like them, what are we doing? Well, whatever we call it, it certainly is not trusting, is it? Wouldn't I say, if I really were trusting, "Leave it all quietly to God, my soul"?

Real trust means going all the way, leaving it quietly to God. An old book called "The Christian Secret of a Happy Life," by Hannah Whitall Smith, has an inspiring thought in it. Trust, to that author of beautiful thoughts, means complete abandonment. Complete abandonment of all interests to God. She says that we should pay no attention to how we feel about it. Emotional sensation, as we might call it, has nothing to do with it. We just trust, that's all. We *leave* it all qui-

Successful Trusting 125

etly to God. We *abandon* our interests to—God's care. And since He has said that He will look out for them, and keep them safe, and forward them for us, why, they will be looked out for, kept safe, and forwarded no matter how we happen to be feeling about it.

If I had some money to deposit in the bank, would it make any difference so far as the safety of that money is concerned whether I happened to feel enthusiastic, or a little "low," at the moment when I deposited it? Well, what difference does it make how I *feel* when I deposit all my cares with God, so long as I deposit them?

The secret of successful trusting, letting go, lies in leaving it lovingly in God's hands, in relying with all our heart, in leaving it all quietly to God—doesn't it? In abandon? No matter how we feel? Try it. One sure thing is that it is the secret of peace. It is the secret of efficiency. It is the secret of power. It is the secret of achievement up to the limit of our possibilities. I can only do my best, when I have peace of mind. I can have peace of mind only when I stop worrying. I can stop worrying only when I have hope. I can have hope only when my interests are safe. And my interests are safe only with—God.

Good "Bad" News

BAD NEWS is what seems to upset us most in our efforts to live a triumphant life. We try to fulfill the conditions we think God lays down, and then we begin to look forward to receiving the promised blessings. When the particular thing we hope for does not materialize at the particular time we hope to get it, we get disappointed and disheartened, rebellious, or frightened, and in a panic we turn away from our faith and grasp at doubt—as if doubt were a refuge when faith fails!

I knew a man who had a fine position in New York. He was the editor of a fiction magazine, a position he had always wanted to have; and his salary was better than any other salary he had ever had. He lived in a suburb, had a very comfortable house to live in; and nice furniture, and congenial neighbors, and many interesting friends. His work was easy, and he loved it. He was popular and looked up to. He had settled into what seemed a satisfactory career, with every evidence that it was permanent. It gave him opportunity to write as an avocation, which was the one thing he wanted most to do. His writings were being accepted and paid for at good rates, and published in good papers and magazines. He was a man to be envied, he thought.

Then suddenly, out of a clear sky, one day he received a note from his employer, the publisher, telling him that his services would not be needed after the following week. He was ousted from his comfortable job. His fine salary stopped. He had to give up his comfortable home. He had to move away from his congenial friends and neighbors. He looked upon that note from his employer which began all this change of circumstances for him as "bad" news, very, very bad news.

He had to leave New York, where he liked to live. He went wandering about the country, trying to make a living by writing, and trying to find a cheap place to live, because his earnings were small. Hard times came along, and the magazines to which he had formerly consistently sold his writings began to curtail their buying, and his market vanished. He got poorer and poorer. Every time one of his stories was declined by an editor who formerly bought his stories, he thought it was bad news. Every time he read a newspaper, he found statements about the hard times in it, and he thought that was bad news too.

He settled in a small town in up State New York where he seemed to find conditions that suited his purposes. He was just beginning to get well started there in making friends, and was beginning to hope that he might weather the hard times there, because expenses were low, and that he might ultimately succeed in his writing there, because it was interesting country and material for stories was abundant, when he came into very unfortunate conflict with a man who immediately took a dislike to him. This man had influence enough in the town to make it very uncomfortable for him to stay there. So this writer-editor felt that he had to move again, and again he looked upon the episode that caused that necessity as very, very "bad news."

He went to another small town, a hundred miles away, and tried to start again. But bad news seemed to pursue him. Still his stories would not sell, still the times were hard. Then one day he met a motion-picture producer who was making a series of pictures up there in the countryside, and who needed just such a man as our editor-writer was. The motion-picture man hired the writing man and things seemed rosy indeed. The work was novel and interesting, and the pay was better than any the writer had previously received.

Everything went well for a few weeks. Then suddenly one day the motion-picture company came to the end of its contract with the firm that distributed its product, and the contract was not renewed. Bad news in the shape of discharge from employment came once more into the writing man's experience. Bad news. Bad news!

But the motion-picture producer gave the writing man a letter of recommendation, which he took back to New York—where he got into another motion-picture company. Presently his salary began to increase, and his authority to rise, and his position to become more important.

Good "Bad" News

Inside of a year he was getting more than twice as much salary as he had received as an editor. Inside of two years his salary was more than three times as much as he had received as an editor. Year by year his income increased. In three years his income had multiplied to five times its original proportions, and when six years had passed, his income was nearly ten times that which had been paid him in the position from which he had been discharged.

Now, all other questions aside, where was the "bad" news? If he had not been discharged from his comfortable editorial berth, he would not have been foot-loose. If he had not been forced to reduce his expenditures, he would not have gone to the country. If he had not been virtually driven out of one town by the ill will of an "enemy," he would not have gone to the town where the motion-picture company was at work. If he had not failed to sell his stories to the magazines, he would never have taken a first job in the movies; and if the first job in the movies had not come suddenly to an end, he would never have gotten the later, bigger ones. "Bad news?" What is bad news?

This sounds like a chapter of accidents. But its meaning seems fairly clear. Bad news may not be bad news at all. It may be good news. It depends on how you look at it. It depends on how long you look at it. It depends on what you do with it, what you do about it. Instead of taking news that disappoints us or postpones events for which we are wishing as bad news, why not look more closely to discover just what it means? Why not take it for granted that it is good news? "Good 'bad' news," we may call it, if we are permitted to be whimsical. Why not take it for granted that all news is merely directions for the road that we want to travel. When you are driving cross-country, you come to a stop sign. You don't think that is bad news, do you? Of course it isn't. It is merely the best way of telling you that you have come to a highway, where the best way to avoid an accident is to stop till you are sure the road is clear for you to go ahead. Or you come to the top of a steep hill, and the safest thing to do is to go into second gear and go down slowly. Or maybe you have come upon a detour sign. Is that bad news? Maybe it seems so sometimes. But it simply tells you that a side road is the best way to get where you want to go. The detour and the stop may seem to delay you, but not so long as getting stuck in mud or sand, or turning back from a washed-out bridge, or having an accident would delay you. So the signs are good "bad" news.

A large part of the news we get seems bad to us at first. But if we will look upon it as good, it will turn out to be good. There is an old saying, "It is an ill wind that blows nobody good." It might be changed to read, truthfully, "It is an ill wind that does not blow good in the end." Paul says, "Overcome evil with good." Did you ever think of overcoming bad news with good? that is, by just seeing it as good news from the start—

surprising good news sometimes, of course, but nevertheless good. You will be astonished how suddenly and surely all bad news will be transformed into good news when you are determined to see it that way.

Some one has said that we should look upon every event in life as a "heavenly messenger" sent direct to us to show us the way to go or what to do to realize our heart's desires. That is one of the wisest and best of all sayings. Calling these messengers or messages "good 'bad' news" is just a way of making the idea arresting, thought-provoking, memorable. It doesn't matter what we call news, if we see it as good. No matter what the news is, if the weather man says rain, if the letter that we looked for does not come, if the decision is against our hopes, if the bank fails, if the doctor shakes his head, just stop, look, and listen, and the real meaning of it will show itself. "Bad" news? What shall I do about it? Get still and think about it quietly! Intuition and inspiration will surely throw light upon it that will transform its whole appearance, that will open it up in beauty as the sun opens a flower.

Harvest

"WHAT WILL you have? quoth God; pay for it and take it," writes Emerson in his essay on compensation. And again,

Men suffer all their life long under the foolish superstition that they can be cheated. But it is as impossible for a man to be cheated by any one but himself, as for a thing to be and not to be at the same time. There is a third silent party to all our bargains. The nature and soul of things takes on itself the guaranty of the fulfillment of every contract, so that honest service cannot come to loss. If you serve an ungrateful master, serve him the more. Put God in your debt. Every stroke shall be repaid. The longer the payment is withholden, the better for you; for compound interest on compound interest is the rate and usage of this exchequer.

Other sages have said the same thing in other terms. But always the tenor of the teaching of great students of life is that you shall be recompensed for what you do in terms of your heart's desire. Somewhere else Emerson says something to the effect that the good man "cannot escape his good." In the 3d chapter of Proverbs, Solomon bears witness, "he blesses the good man's dwelling," and "wise men come to honour." In the 4th chapter "the course of good men, like a ray of dawn, shines on and on to the full light of day." In the 10th chapter "the Eternal never stints an honest man" and "the hopes of good men end in bliss." In the 11th chapter "the path of a right-minded man is cleared by his own goodness" and "the good man is brought safe out of adversity." I quote from Moffatt's translation, because the words in modern language become suddenly striking sometimes, when passages from the older versions seem overfamiliar.

Quotations could be multiplied almost endlessly. Besides the ones I have mentioned there are many more in succeeding chapters of Proverbs. There are many in The Psalms. Moses said the same thing, as did Isaiah. So did the ancient writers of the Vedas, and Confucius, and Lao-tse. In one form or another all the sages of all the ages have told us that God wants us to have what we desire. How do they—or did they—know? By experience, of course—by observation—by revelation. Just as we can know if we will fulfill one condition. As Kingsley said, "Be good . . . and let who will be clever." That's the single condition of our finding out. We don't have to take Emerson's word, or Solomon's, or Lao-tse's.

The proverbs of a people always contain the distilled wisdom of its great men. No proverb that is not true can live very long. "Be good and be happy" is a proverb. It has been ridiculed endlessly, but it is still alive because it is still true. It is a demonstrable axiom.

But we have a habit of thinking that maybe there's some kind of catch in promises like that

—some kind of string tied to them. We think, "Oh, yes, we shall be happy if we are good—happy with so-called spiritual happiness—not with satisfaction in earthly achievement or possessions." But when we think such a thing as that, we are virtually calling the world's sages cheats and swindlers and confidence men; which they are not, and never were. They meant what they said, exactly as they said it.

Cowards have twisted the old promises, and explained them, and perverted them, and hedged them about with if's and and's and peradventure's and maybe's and perhaps's because they have not dared to claim these promises for themselves; because they have not wanted to fulfill the conditions; because they shrank from committing themselves; because they feared the sneers of doubters and skeptics. Sometimes even preachers in the pulpits of our churches sidestep the promises, dodge any statement of belief in them, undertake to explain that they do not mean what they say— that they mean something else. But the honest man who reads the Bible with clear eyes and an open mind cannot escape the fact that it is packed with promises of recompense for plain goodness in terms of his heart's desires.

"Ask whatsoever ye will." "Whatsoever ye shall ask in my name." "We shall reap, if we faint not." "Whatsoever he doeth shall prosper." Take the Good Book and thumb it over with some notion that it actually means what is says, that it records the genuine experiences of men with

God. You will find that it sets forth what we could say with all reverence, in modern parlance, is a "square-shooting God"—"a God of His word."

But better even than thumbing through the Bible is putting it to the test. Have you ever tried making a soft answer to an irate traffic officer? Have you ever tried doing the fellow a good turn who has been trying to injure you? Have you ever tried promoting the interests of a rival? Have you ever let the other fellow have the credit that rightfully belonged to you? If you have, can you honestly say that so-called spiritual satisfaction is the only recompense you have received? That's a challenge. Answer it! Not to me, of course—to your own heart.

Do you know why we sometimes think no reward comes from doing right—just plain right, without regard to anything else? It is because we look for some immediate return from the person or persons who receive the benefit of our act or acts. That's why. We take too narrow a view. We forget about the "bread cast upon the waters." We overlook the dollars-and-cents value of reputation, of "repeat business," of the satisfied customer, of commercial credit.

The fact is that very seldom does the return come from the person we have benefited, or on the day of the benefit, or in the same form as the right deed. If for no other purpose, some of us should keep diaries to record our efforts to do right and the course our lives take subsequently. Sometimes the results are as obscure as some of the workings of nature. Snow melts on a mountain top, and somewhere miles below bubbles up a spring. The glacier deposits soil that some day becomes a fertile countryside. A beetle we look upon as a nuisance destroys an unrecognized parasite pest.

I "trust in the Lord, and do good" today; and tomorrow in some emergency He directs my paths. I am merely kind today; and tomorrow somebody does me a special favor that more than balances the scales. If not tomorrow, maybe next week. Maybe next year. But, somebody objects, next year is too long to wait. Why so? "In the morning sow thy seed, and in the evening withhold not thy hand; for thou knowest not which shall prosper, whether this or that, or whether they both shall be alike good." If I want my good to be a steady inflowing stream I must keep on doing good steadily. I should be a merchant of many enterprises, all going at once and all eventually bringing back their meed of profit. Living is a marvelous enterprise. Right living brings a marvelous return even during depressions. In the bright lexicon of Truth there is no such word as depression!

God is no trickster. He is as honest with you and me as we are with ourselves. Yes, and much more honest. Basil King in his "Conquest of Fear" calls Him the greatest of all paymasters, and says, "He pays me, and He pays me well. He will not fail to pay me." And God's standard of reward is "abundantly above all that we ask or think."

Spiritual reward? Certainly. That's the best part. But with "all these things . . . added." I think I have written elsewhere that it sometimes seems to me we ought to reverse our usual procedure. Instead of trying to provide material things for ourselves and leaving God to look after our spiritual affairs, we should attend to our spiritual affairs and let God take care of our material interests. Is not that exactly what He asks us to do? Isn't that what Jesus meant when He said, "Seek ye first his kingdom . . . and all these things shall be added" and "Your heavenly Father knoweth that ye have need of all these things"? Oh ye of little faith! Do you think God delights to befool you? Answer that!—not to me—in your own heart. Well, if not, then why not try this: "Bring ye the whole tithe [good deeds] into the store-house . . . and prove me [God] now herewith . . . if I will not open you the windows of heaven, and pour you out a blessing, that there shall not be room enough *to receive it.*" That's a challenge too! Why not take it up? Then you won't need to be guided by the sayings of other wise men. You yourself will be wise. You will know.

My Own Will Come to Me

ALL MY LIFE I have known in a vague way that getting money is the result of earning it, but I have never had a perfect vision of that fact till recently. If I give to anybody service of a kind that he wants, I shall get back the benefit myself. If I give more service, I shall get more benefit. If I give a great deal more, I shall get a great deal more. But I shall get back more than I give. If I give more to my employer than he expects of me, he will give me a raise—and on no other condition. What is more, his giving me a raise does not depend on his fair-mindedness. He has to give it to me or lose me, because if he does not appreciate me somebody else will.

But this is only part of it. If I give help to the man whose desk is next to mine, it will come back to me multiplied, even if he is apparently a rival. What I give to him I give to the firm, and the firm will value it, because it is teamwork in the organization that the firm primarily wants, not brilliant individual performance.

If I have an enemy in the organization, the same rule holds. If I give him, with the purpose of helping him, something that will genuinely help him, I am giving service to the organization. Great corporations appreciate the peacemaker, for a prime requisite in their success is harmony among employees. If my immediate boss is unappreciative the same rule holds. If I give him more in advance of appreciation, he cannot ultimately withhold his appreciation and keep his own job.

The more you think about this law the deeper you will see it goes. It literally hands you a blank check, signed by the maker of universal law, and leaves you to fill in the amount and the kind of payment you want! Mediocre successes are those of men who obey this law a little way, who fill in the check with a small amount, but who stop short of big vision in doing it. If every employee would only get the idea of this law firmly fixed in his mind as a principle not subject to wavering with fluctuating moods, the success of the organization would be miraculous. One of my fears is apt to be that by promoting the other fellow's success, I am sidetracking my own; but the exact opposite is true.

Suppose every employee would look at his own case as an exact parallel to that of his firm. What does his firm give for the money it gets from the public? Service! Service in advance! The better the service that is given out the more is the money that comes back. What does the firm do to bring public attention to its service? It advertises; that is part of the service. Now, suppose that I, as an employee, begin giving my services to the firm in advance of all hoped-for payment. I cannot do anything constructive in that firm's office or store or plant or premises that is not service—from filing a letter correctly to mending the fence or pleasing a customer; from looking up a word for the stenographer to encouraging her to look it up herself; from demonstrating a machine to a customer to encouraging him to demononstrate it himself; from helping my immediate apparent rival to get a raise to selling the whole season's output.

As for advertising myself, I begin advertising myself the moment I walk into the office or the store or the shop in the morning; I cannot help it. Everybody who looks at me sees my advertisement. Everybody around me has my advertisement before his eyes all day long. So has the boss, my immediate chief, and the head of the firm, no matter where they are. And if I live up to my advertising, nobody can stop me from selling my goods—my services! The more a man knocks me, the more he advertises me, because he calls attention to me; and if I am delivering something better than he says I am, the interested parties—my employers—will see it and will not be otherwise influenced by what he says.

More than that, I must *give* to every human being I come in contact with, from my wife to the bootblack who shines my shoes, from my brother to my sworn foe. Sometimes people tell me to smile; but the smile I give must be a real smile that lives up to its advertising. If I go around grinning like a Cheshire cat; the Cheshire-cat grin will be what I get back—multiplied! If I give the real thing, I'll get the real thing back—multiplied!

My Own Will Come to Me

If anybody objects that this is a selfish view to take, I answer him that any law of salvation from anything that has ever been offered by anybody for any purpose offers a selfish view. The only unselfishness that has ever been taught truly is that of giving a lesser thing in the hope of receiving a greater!

Now, why am I so sure of this law? How can you be sure? I have been watching it work; it works everywhere. I believe you have only to try it, and keep on trying it, and it will prove true for you. It is not true because I say so, nor because anybody else says so; it is just true. Theosophists call it the law of karma; humanitarians call it the law of service; business men call it the law of common sense; Jesus Christ called it the law of love. It rules whether I know it or not, whether I believe it or not, whether I defy it or not. I cannot break it!

Now, without referring to any religious idea you may have about Jesus of Nazareth, without considering whether He was or was not divine, recall that He spoke these words: "Give, and it shall be given unto you; good measure, pressed down, shaken together, running over." And this appears certainly to be so; not because He said it, not because God Himself has said it; but because it is Truth, which we all, whether we admit it or not, worship as God. No man can honestly say that he does not put the truth supreme. It is true, this principle of giving and receiving, only there are few men who go the limit on it. But going the limit is the way to unlimited returns!

Well, then, what shall I give? What I have, of course. Suppose you believe in this idea, and suppose you start giving it out—the idea itself—tactfully, wisely; and start living it yourself in your business organization. How long do you think it will be before you are a power in that organization, recognized as such and getting pay as such? If this idea is true, it is more valuable than all the cleverness and special information you can possibly possess without it. What you have, give—to everybody. If you have an idea, do not save it for your own use only; give it. It is the best thing you have to give and therefore the thing that will bring the best back to you.

I begin to suspect that if a man would follow this principle, even to his trade secrets, he would profit steadily more and more; and more certainly than he will by holding on to anything exclusively for himself. He would never have to worry about his own affairs, because he would be working on the basis of fundamental law. Law never fails, and it will be easy for you to discover what is or is not law. And if law is worth using part of the time, it is worth using all the time.

Look around you first with an eye to seeing the truth, and then put the thing to the test. If our reasoning is sound, through both methods of investigation you will find a blank check waiting for you to fill in with "whatsoever ye pray and ask for" and a new way to pray and to get what you pray for!

When I Am Unaware——

I HEARD A WONDERFUL sermon once on the subject of unconscious influence.

The idea expressed was that whatever influence we have on others or in the world at large will always be almost wholly unknown to us. Our unconscious influence will always be as much greater than our conscious influence as the proverbial part of the iceberg under water is greater than that above the surface; as much greater as my so-called subconscious mind is greater than my conscious mind.

How do I know what my influence on the baby in the cradle is, or how far-reaching it is? It may affect him profoundly and extend on throughout his whole life. For good or ill! My harsh word to his mother may lay the foundation for his attitude toward her, toward all women. My love for her, expressed, may set his standard for all his years. I think he is too young to take notice of things. But that is not true. Child specialists have said that a human being's character is largely formed before he is three years old. What part has my unconscious influence in forming it?

How do I know what my influence is on the young man or the young woman who works for me, who applies to me for work? Are these two not affected by my encouragement or my coldness?

Are they not inspired or embittered by what I say, by my manner, by my very attitude?

How do I know what my unconscious influence is on the clerk who waits upon me in the store? Is he or she indifferent to my captious faultfinding or my appreciation of good service? What about the gas-station attendant? Is he influenced by my indifference to his efforts to please me, by my word of thanks? What about my grocer, my barber, my bootblack, my chief clerk, my stenographer, my office boy? What about my employer or my partner? Is it possible that they watch me, each one, and take from me some cue for living? Is it possible that they live just a little differently because of contacts with me? Is it possible that I make them a little more miserable or a little more hopeful and happy because I pass their way?

It has often been said that you can tell what a man's mood is by the way he blows the horn on the car. He is impatient, he is arrogant, he is ugly; he is courteous, he is considerate, he is kind. Can he tell what I am like by the way I blow my horn? Of course he can. He is just as intelligent and as open to impressions as I am. He is just as susceptible to "passing" influence.

How am I affected by other people's unconscious influence? Why, some people have affected the whole course of my life without being aware of it at all! There was the teacher in primary school or kindergarten who chose me to do an errand for her because my hair was brushed! There

When I Am Unaware—— 145

was the cousin who told me my nose was atrociously big! There was the crowd that laughed when I ran after a foul ball that flew up over my boyish head as I watched a high-school game—and muffed it. There was the drunken man who passed my home when I was five, and staggered along with one foot off and one foot on the sidewalk. There was the man with the broken arm who sat and let the doctor set it, laughing and telling stories throughout the operation, while I watched in awe and admiration. There was the employer who always stopped talking when I burst in with something I wanted to say. There was the young man who kissed his father after a separation and was unashamed of affection before a hotel crowd. There was the college professor who gave me a second examination after I had flunked because he knew I could pass. There was the father who taught me to shovel the snow off the walk *clean* so that nobody else would have to sweep it after me. There was the mother who forgave me for lying to her and made me everlastingly ashamed of being untrue. There was the wife who believed in my ability to make good when I was apparently failing. There was the rival who quit in my favor and congratulated me on my success. There was the workman who admired my wonderful dad and made me appreciate him. There was the sister who thought I was much more generous than I am and made me want to live up to her opinion of me.

Some of these people perhaps tried to influence

me a little. None of them realized how deep their influence went, and how after all the years I remember, and remember—and am spurred to new efforts because of those memories.

Do you ever wake up in the night and remember the contacts of the day, or the contacts of yesterday or last year, or of childhood? Do you think those memories have no influence on you? Do you think the other people involved know that you are still thinking about those contacts with them?

What do you suppose those people got out of the contacts with you? Do you know? Of course you don't. You think that they forget you. Well, they don't. They are just like you. They wake up in the night and think. Their hearts go down or their spirits rise because of something you did or said or looked, just as your courage ebbs or flows because of something they gave you. A word, an act, a glance, an attitude, a sigh, a laugh, a sob, a mean trick, an act of self-sacrifice—one of yours—was stamped upon their hearts and souls. Something you did, something you said, something you were, now makes them set their teeth and clench their hands, or shrug and laugh, or cower and shrink, or give and give. Think not? Well, you are much more important, then, than you know.

God put you where you are, to be a channel for His messages to somebody, to everybody, to all around you. You can't live and breathe and work and play without influencing the people all around you. Would it not be marvelous if that influence could only be a help and an inspiration always? How could you make it so?

It is often said that we cannot consciously influence people very much. Why? Is it because the portion of ourselves that we are most conscious of is the portion that influences them least? Is it because "what you are . . . thunders so that I cannot hear what you say"? Might it not be better if we stopped trying to be conscious of our influence and let the unconscious influence do the work? Perhaps you will ask yourself if I am consciously trying to influence you by what I am saying here. Well, whatever what I say is worth, you will be more influenced by something I am not aware of saying.

Of course we try consciously to influence one another. If you know that there is a washout in the road, you will try to warn me of it. I may accept your warning and benefit by it, but you will never know that you have shamed me by the contrast between your thoughtfulness and my usual selfish indifference to the welfare of others, and that next time I am going to emulate you. Do you suppose the good Samaritan had any idea that the Christ would hold his simple kindness up to the world as an example of what it is to be a good neighbor? Even if Jesus' parable about him was only fiction, Jesus had in mind some prototype who actually did something of the kind. So that prototype was unconscious of the impression he left in the mind of the Master.

Perhaps the reason why my unconscious influence is always greater than my conscious influence is that what I unconsciously show of my intention is always sincere. It is sincerity that influences people. Sincerity cuts deep. It convinces the mind and wrings the heart. It makes indelible impressions. It burns. Why? Because sincerity is Truth—and Truth is God. When good is expressed through me, it is God's own self finding expression. Of course it cuts deep and wrings and burns, and leaves an ineffaceable memory. Is not the best way to make my unconscious influence always helpful, always good, just to forget about conscious attempts to exert influence and let God attend to it? If I just try to express Him, He will attend to it.

What else have I to do in life but to express Him? If I do, my influence will take care of itself. And consciously letting God express Himself through me, think what may be my unconscious influence upon myself!

WORKING WITH GOD

You Can't Beat Spiritual Law

THE LAW IS that what I give out comes back to me multiplied. Then the way to success of any kind, as I may convince myself by experience, is to begin giving out what I want to have come back. If I have no money, obviously I cannot give money. But money is the mere symbol of service, and I can always give service of some kind.

The way for me to give is to give something that I have to the person nearest to me who needs it most, without expectation of return from him or her, knowing that God is my paymaster and that He is the best of all paymasters. "He will pay me and He will pay me well; He will not fail to pay me," writes Basil King. He will begin paying me when I begin working exclusively for Him. He will not let me work on and on without any encouragement or sign of His approval, just to see how long I can stand it. He will give me the help I need, because He cannot help giving it. He too conforms to the law, because He *is* the law. Let us try to remember, you and I, that we are working with real law all the time. If you turn on the electric current, you get light or heat, because you are obeying a law. If you obey the law you cannot help getting light or heat. Well, if you turn on the law of giving, you cannot help receiving, can you?

The greatest blessing that ever came into my life—and I mean concrete, material blessing, too, and not some imaginary or vague uplift of spirit—came when I took up a bit of service I was asked to perform at a time when I was in what I thought desperate straits for material things. It looked as if there was not a chance in the world that any money would come to me as a result of this service. It was not a service for which money is paid. I have never been paid for it in money. As I continued in the service I did not see that it produced any opportunity to get money. All that it produced was the opportunity to give more unremunerative service. Plenty of people were willing to have me serve them in certain ways. But I had made up my mind that giving was the way to receiving, and I had the sense to stick to it—or I may better say, I was led to stick to it simply because I was trying to find out how to obey the law. I thought it was not going to pay. I was accustomed to saying that I had tried everything and that nothing produced for me, and I grew discouraged and desperate. But all the time I got along; I was taken care of—in what I thought little ways and ways that did not satisfy me, to be sure; but I was encouraged to go on serving.

Emerson says: "If you serve an ungrateful master, serve him the more. Put God in your debt. Every stroke shall be repaid. The longer

You Can't Beat Spiritual Law

the payment is withholden, the better for you; for compound interest on compound interest is the rate and usage of this exchequer." I read that over and over and learned it and repeated it and thought it and believed it. Then I learned by heart what Jesus says: "Give, and it shall be given unto you." And I repeated that, and repeated it, and believed it, and stuck to my giving—giving everything I had to the thing I was called upon to do.

I am not setting myself up as a model for you. I am simply telling you about a method that did for me what you want done for you. It is like repeating to you a recipe for bread that I once found made good bread, and telling you that it will make good bread for you also if you will follow it exactly. This was my experience when I began to give service: Presently things began to come to me in unexpected ways from sources that to all appearances were entirely unconnected with the work I was doing, and I began to get fulfillment of my heart's desires. I cannot detail all the things that happened to me; but I can tell you this: I found that the way out of an individual trouble is exactly what Jesus says it is. Why not follow it just as carefully as you would follow a bread recipe? that is, put in all the ingredients in full measure. For "with what measure ye mete, it shall be measured unto you." Just let go of worry, and believe that the law is going to work. It is; because when people are really willing to do all they really know as their share, if it is law, it never fails to work.

Let us apply the principle. Does not your own experience teach you that it will prove itself? If you want a job, begin giving service somewhere along that line. Let us see; God says that if you will commit your ways to Him, He will direct your paths. If you do not know what vocation you should be in, give your services along any line, and your particular line will open to you. "Whatsoever he doeth shall prosper." So you will find everything that your heart desires: health, money, friends, success, the development of your talents, home, prosperity, love, happiness. For God, if He is law, does not stint anybody. God is the law of love, and He loves you. He sets you the example that He wants you to follow; He gives, gives lavishly, regardless of return, patiently, joyously. Suppose we try His method. Imitate God. He knows how to obey His own law, because He is the law itself!

I do not mean to preach at you. As a matter of fact, I am merely rejoicing on paper that this is all true and that it has been given me to find it out. The blessing of finding it out came through practicing the law of giving and receiving at a time when I seemed not to have a thing in the world to give except an idea or two that I thought somebody else might use. I mean to continue to practice the application of this law, just as I practice paying my fare on the trolley line knowing I shall get a ride. Both laws work in

You Can't Beat Spiritual Law

the same way. They do! And they never "slip up," if I may use such an expression for the sake of emphasis. Never! Never! They cannot. Things are made that way! Seeds grow to plants when they are planted. All the service that you give out brings its return. These are your planting: deeds, words, thoughts—everything.

"Now Is the Accepted Time"

"BE YE THEREFORE PERFECT," Jesus said. That seems a hard saying, doesn't it? Because we look upon perfection as a goal so far beyond us.

But He added, "Even as your Father which is in heaven is perfect." Isn't this the clue to our approach to the ideal? If we let God express Himself through us, will the result fall short of perfection? "The Father abiding in me doeth his works."

There is a fragment of a verse somewhere that says, "Having done all, to stand." Doesn't that mean that, having let go and placed our problem lovingly in the hands of the Father, leaving it all quietly to God, we shall find ourselves arriving at contentment, happiness, peace? And the greatest of these is peace.

With worry forgotten, anxiety stilled, and fear forever done away with, what can heart desire beyond the resulting peace? Peace is the secret of achievement, the root soil of love, the prerequisite of union with the indwelling Christ. When human hearts know peace, they overflow with joy.

Peace is not mere passivity, resignation, inactivity. It is utter well-being, conscious and unconscious. Peace is heaven. Must we wait till the world is at peace, till crime and war and sin vanish from the earth, before you and I can have peace? Certainly not. Peace is an atmosphere of the heart, a state of the individual soul, and has nothing to do with environment or circumstance.

"A thousand shall fall at thy side,
 And ten thousand at thy right hand,
 But it shall not come nigh thee."

The 91st Psalm tells what peace is. It is dwelling "in the secret place of the Most High."

We all know what peace is, even if only from momentary experiences of it. It is the priceless *summum bonum* toward which our heart forever yearns. Yet it is within our reach, yours and mine, if we are only content, "having done all, to stand."

If we are committed to a life of giving, a life of loving, a life of being—of being an open channel—peace is the inevitable result. When we begin that life, peace begins. As we grow into that life, peace grows into us. Perhaps it will take a completed eternity to open every channel to God and find complete peace. But we can find a "peace of God, which passeth all understanding" now.

"Now is the accepted time." It is the accepted time for beginning to live, for beginning to love, for beginning to give, for beginning to enjoy. Everything God asks of us, everything God promises us is for the eternal now. We think it will take time, at best, to get what we want. How long would it take to become galvanized if you should take hold of a live wire? God is a live wire, and heaven is the current that flows through Him. Does it shock you to think in such simple terms of God? Why? Isn't electricity one of the manifestations of God's power? God tells us to think simply—as simply as a child.

"But," you say, "not all of God's laws work instantaneously. We are told about planting and waiting for the harvest."

That illustrates one phase of working with God. I spoke of the live wire to illustrate another phase. Time concerns matters of material, earthly things. For food and clothes and houses and money I may have to wait awhile. But for the big things I do not have to wait at all. If I begin really to work with God, the instantaneous result is love. If I really, actually leave all results quietly to God, the instantaneous result is peace. The instantaneous result of peace is joy. What do I think food and clothing and houses and money will give me, anyway? Will they give me love and peace and joy?

It is only the arrival of the things "added" that takes time. The coming of the kingdom is instantaneous—the instant we seek. "Ye shall seek me, and find me, when ye shall search for me with all your heart." When? "When ye shall search for me." The addition of the things that my Heavenly Father knows I have need of will follow —inevitably.

"But isn't it going to take time for me to do the things referred to in the phrase 'Having done all, to stand' '"?

Yes, if you think so. But why should you think it takes time to "leave it all quietly to God"? That is all you have to do.

"But I have to love my enemies. Won't that take time?"

Of course—if you think so. But suppose you leave all that quietly to God?

"But won't it take time for me to begin to love?"

If you think so, yes. But if you turn to God with the thought of loving them that despitefully use you, before you ask He will answer.

"Then it is all a matter of my thinking? I don't know how to think right. It will take time for me to learn—if I ever do."

Will it? Why not leave all that quietly to God? That's right thinking—isn't it?

"But wait a minute! Won't it take time for me to begin to give?"

The essence of giving is in the thought of giving, isn't it? We've discussed the time it takes to think.

"Well, anyway, it is going to take time for me to receive."

"All things whatsoever the Father hath are mine." Do you want tomorrow's food today?

"But I want health today."

Why not leave it all quietly to God?

"But perhaps I find it impossible to believe all these beautiful things."

Why not leave that quietly to God?

You see, you can't "poke holes" in Truth. It is unanswerable. All it demands of you is to try it. You find it hard only because you have the habit of believing something else. Anticipating your question, I answer that it doesn't take time to break a habit if you will put it lovingly in the hands of the Father.

John Burroughs wrote a fine poem which he called "Waiting." Here is the first stanza:

> "Serene, I fold my hands and wait,
>   Nor care for wind, or tide, or sea;
> I rave no more 'gainst time or fate,
>   For, lo! my own shall come to me."

Are we not all much too much concerned with activities in the material world? When we think of giving, why not think of the best things we have to give? Love, for instance. Prayer, for instance. If we remember that everything that ultimately becomes manifest in the material world begins first in thought, that removes a mountain of difficulties, doesn't it?

Perhaps we are afraid or ashamed to commit ourselves to a life of faith and trust and love. We think perhaps we may be disappointed and become ridiculous. What do we mean by committing ourselves? Telling somebody else we are going to try it? What do we mean by becoming ridiculous? In somebody else's eyes? Well, why tell anybody what we are trying to do? Why risk the ridicule? We do not have to advertise our undertaking. We do not have to risk anything.

Indeed, the less we advertise it the better.

But if we really do begin the life of "working with God," we shall forget all about advertising and risks. To be sure, what we are doing will advertise itself—in results. Instead of ridicule, we shall promptly have large numbers of people around us asking us what has happened to us— how we do it—how they can do it too. We shall have something to give, we shall find it easy to love, we shall gain wisdom, we shall see multiform opportunities on all sides of us, we shall achieve.

And there shall be added unto us "exceeding abundantly above all that we ask or think." Because, when we begin working with God, God works with us—and God works miracles.